Understanding a Company's Finances

Understanding a Company's Finances

A GRAPHIC APPROACH

W. R. Purcell, Jr.

BARNES & NOBLE BOOKS
A DIVISION OF HARPER & ROW, PUBLISHERS
New York, Cambridge, Philadelphia, San Francisco,
London, Mexico City, São Paulo, Sydney

A hardcover edition of this book is published by Houghton Mifflin Company. It is here reprinted by arrangement.

First BARNES & NOBLE BOOKS edition published 1983.

Library of Congress Cataloging in Publication Data

Purcell, W.R. (W. Richard)
    Understanding a company's finances.

    Reprint. Originally published: Boston : Houghton Mifflin, 1981.
    1. Financial statements. 2. Corporations—Finance—Charts, diagrams, etc. I. Title.
HG4028.B2P8   1983   658.1'5   83-47597
ISBN 0-06-463583-X (pbk.)

83 84 85 86 87 10 9 8 7 6 5 4 3 2 1

Acknowledgments

IN A BROAD SENSE, this book represents a new application to
business finance of an approach that has long been used very
effectively for teaching and communication in many other
fields, such as engineering and geography: the use of diagrams
to explain a subject by showing how its parts fit together. So in
a broad sense I owe thanks to those who pioneered the use of
diagrams to explain other subjects.

A continuing series of two-day courses that I conduct for
accountants, under sponsorship of the American Institute of
Certified Public Accountants, has given me a superb oppor-
tunity to test and refine the system of diagrams of business
finance in this book. I want to express my appreciation to the
AICPA and the following AICPA personnel: Stacy Kosmides
and Anne Tucksmith, who have directly managed most of this
course series; Joseph Cote, Carole Fishman, and George Adair
who played key roles in launching or guiding the course series;
and Rex Cruse who directs the entire AICPA continuing
education program.

At Houghton Mifflin, Richard McAdoo guided the development of this book, providing a marvelous blend of encourage-
ment and constructive suggestions. In a similarly helpful way
Larry Kessenich coordinated its preparation for publication,
and Edward Reynolds, Craig Wylie, and Austin Olney all contributed to its development.

Frank Laskowski of the Columbus College of Art and Design prepared the final art for all illustrations. He devoted himself totally to making the illustrations as clear and effective as possible. He has done a marvelous job — his art makes the diagrams as helpful as they could possibly be.

Far more than to anyone else I owe a debt of gratitude to Shirley Santo Schick. Over the ten years that this book and its underlying materials have been in development, she has typed and retyped many thousands of draft pages, and handled an unlimited array of related and unrelated administrative matters so that I could focus on developing and testing the diagrams and writing the book. Without her this book would not exist.

Contents

Preface

THIS BOOK shows people how to *understand* company financial reports.

I've found, in conducting dozens of short courses on this topic, that most investors and managers do not really understand financial reports at all, even after reading several books or taking several courses on the subject. Even company presidents.

This is a terrible situation. A company's financial reports provide a marvelously comprehensive and concise picture of its progress and status. They contain information that is extremely important to people who invest in companies, and even more important to the people who make a company's plans and decisions.

Furthermore, the financial report system is superbly logical, and easy to understand if it is explained well. What has kept most investors and managers from understanding financial reports is that the traditional methods of explaining them are dreadful — they explain the financial report system as a lot of separate bits and pieces, when the key to understanding it is seeing how it all fits together.

I've found, in teaching my short courses, that people without any knowledge of finance or accounting *can* learn to understand financial reports, and in only a few hours. The secret is to show people how all the parts of a company's finances fit together, in a financial picture that is completely logical and easy to understand quickly.

That is just what this book does.

The book is written for laymen. It is suited for all investors interested in using financial reports in evaluating companies as investments; all professional, managerial, and office people who need or want to understand financial reports in connection with their jobs; all students who may be future managers or investors; and every citizen interested in sharpening his or her understanding of business. This book can also help accountants, finance specialists, and educators, by providing them a good way to explain how the finances of a business operate and how the financial reports reflect them.

W. R. PURCELL, JR.

Understanding a Company's Finances

· 1 ·

Picturing a
Company's Development

ALL THE PARTS of a company's financial reports fit together like the parts of a map. Once you see how they fit together, you can turn the reports into a map of the company's finances.

To illustrate, say that you and I are considering investment in the start-up of a new company, to be named Pump & Paddle Company, that will make and sell inflatable rubber boats. The two people who plan to start and manage the firm have provided us predicted financial reports for the company's first year, which an accountant worked out from their plans for the company. These financial reports include a predicted *income statement* for the company's first year. It looks like this:

INCOME STATEMENT
First Year, in $000

Sales		$300
Expenses		
Cost of goods sold	$108	
Selling expense	75	
Administrative expense	60	
Depreciation	15	
		258
Profit before tax		$ 42
Tax		21
Net profit		$ 21

And they also include a predicted *balance sheet* for start and end of the company's first year, which looks like this:

BALANCE SHEET

Start and End of First Year, in $000

Assets	Start of Year	End of Year	Liabilities & Equity	Start of Year	End of Year
Cash	$ 50	$ 86	Accounts payable	$ 0	$ 0
Accounts receivable	0	0			
Inventory					
Finished goods	18	18			
Work in process	1	1			
Raw materials	6	6			
	$ 25	$ 25			
Equipment	75	60	Stockholders' equity	150	171
Total	$150	$171	Total	$150	$171

These two reports, the income statement and the balance sheet, are the two standard traditional financial reports for any business.

To see how the parts of these two reports all fit together like the parts of a map, look at these two lists of parts for a map of Ohio:

Highways	Cities	
Interstate 70	Akron	Dayton
Interstate 71	Cambridge	Mansfield
Interstate 75	Cincinnati	Marietta
Interstate 76	Cleveland	Toledo
Interstate 77	Columbus	Youngstown
Interstate 80		
Interstate 90		

Of course, the cities listed on the right are where the people are, and the highways listed on the left are routes by which people move among the cities. And by turning these two lists into a map, showing which highways connect which cities...

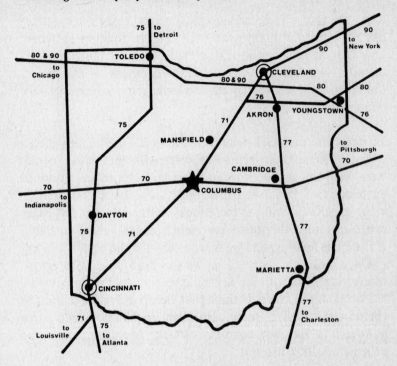

. . . you can see how all the parts of both lists fit together in a picture of Ohio.

With just the lists you could not plan travel in Ohio, but when they are turned into a map you have an excellent basis for understanding Ohio's geography and planning your travel there.

The items listed on the Pump & Paddle financial reports are very much like the highways and cities on the Ohio lists. The Pump & Paddle balance sheet lists categories or places where Pump & Paddle financial value *stops and stays,* like the Ohio cities where people stay. And the items listed on the Pump & Paddle income statement are categories or routes over which Pump & Paddle *moves* value, like the Ohio highways over which people move.

All the routes and places on the financial reports fit together, like the cities and highways on the Ohio map. So by sketching how they fit together we can create a map of the company's finances — a financial picture of the company — that makes the company's finances as easy to understand and read as the Ohio map.

To draw the financial picture of Pump & Paddle, let's sketch rectangular tanks to represent categories that value comes from, stops in, and goes from. Some tanks represent groups of outsiders that Pump & Paddle gets value from and delivers value to, and we will put these tanks at the right and left edges of the picture. Other tanks represent kinds of value that Pump & Paddle is holding, and we will put them in the center column.

Once tanks are sketched in, we can draw pipes with arrowheads to show how Pump & Paddle receives and delivers value.

For example, the first thing that Pump & Paddle will do to get started is collect some cash from stockholders who agree to invest in the new company. In our financial picture the process will look like this:

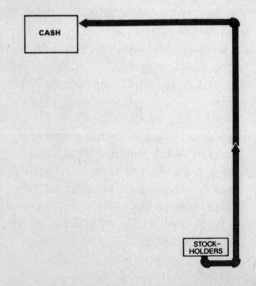

The cash flows from stockholders, a group of outsiders represented by a tank at far right, to Pump & Paddle's own *cash* tank, located in the center column.

The company's second step will be to buy boat-making equipment from suppliers and pay for it. On the sketch, that step will look like this:

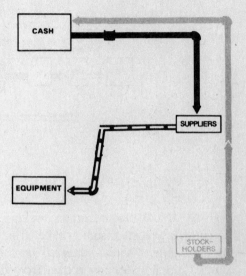

Out from the company's cash tank to a suppliers tank on the right goes the cash payment for the equipment. And in from the suppliers tank to a Pump & Paddle *equipment* tank in the center column comes the equipment.

The inflow of equipment is shown as a dashed pipe, to distinguish it from flows of cash which are shown as solid pipes. We will use dashed pipes for all flows of value in the form of physical goods instead of cash. And we will use dotted pipes to represent flows of value in the form of intangibles, such as services being received from employees.

As its third and final step in preparation for the first year, Pump & Paddle will start boat production and complete some boats for sale. To do so, the company will buy and pay for some rubber from suppliers, and then buy and pay for some work from production employees to turn some of the rubber into completed boats. On the picture the start of production will look like this:

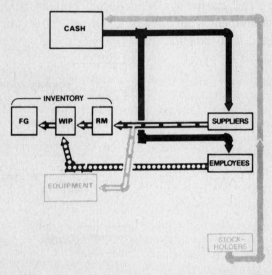

The company receives some rubber from suppliers, which goes into the company's *raw-materials inventory* (RM) tank, and pays the suppliers for this rubber from its cash tank. Then the company moves some of the rubber from raw materials into a *work-in-process* inventory (WIP) tank, which represents boats being made. In turning the rubber into boats, employees add labor value to the boats being made; this is represented by the dotted pipe of labor value flowing from employees to work-in-process inventory. And the company pays cash to the employees for this labor value. Finally, as boats are completed they are moved to a third inventory tank, *finished goods* (FG), which represents completed products ready for sale.

Now Pump & Paddle is ready to begin its first-year operations. The Pump & Paddle tanks in the center column represent the value in various forms that the company now has, and the rest of the picture shows how Pump & Paddle got this value.

· 2 ·

Picturing a
Company's Operation

To MAKE the financial picture of Pump & Paddle reflect the company's first-year operation, we will have to sketch another tank, representing the company's customers. Let's locate this tank in the upper left corner of the picture.

The company will deliver to customers value in the form of boats, and in return receive cash payments from the customers for the boats:

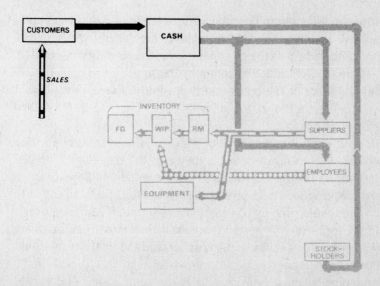

The dashed arrow to customers represents the boat value Pump & Paddle delivers to them, measured at what they agree to pay for the boats. This flow is the company's *sales*.

In order to achieve sales, Pump & Paddle will have to use up value in various ways, such as using up boats it has made and using up work of the sales manager. We can depict the achieving of sales by sketching a "sales pump," like this:

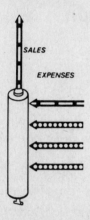

Into the sales pump flow the various kinds of value used up to achieve the sales. The values used up are called *expenses*. And out of the pump to the customers flows the resulting sales value.

One kind of value the company has to use up to help achieve sales is some of the boats that it put into finished goods earlier — see illustration at top of next page. This expense is called *cost of goods sold*.

As the term implies, cost of goods sold represents boats used up for sales in terms of what they cost the company. The picture shows this by indicating where the value that flows through the cost-of-goods-sold pipe comes from. Value gets to the cost-of-goods-sold pipe by coming in from suppliers and employees, in the forms of rubber and labor, and then moving through the three inventory tanks as the rubber and labor are turned into boats. So the boat value that flows through the cost-of-goods-sold pipe when a boat is sold is the same value that earlier

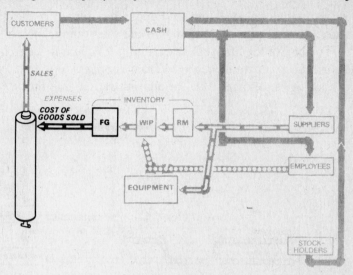

came in as rubber and labor and then was put into making that boat. For example, if the value the company puts into each boat is rubber costing $12 from suppliers and labor costing $6 from employees, this boat enters finished-goods inventory as $18 of boat value, and then flows out as $18 of cost of goods sold when the boat is sold.

In terms of *physical products,* the boats that flow through the cost-of-goods-sold pipe into the pump over any period are the same boats that flow out from the pump to customers as sales over the same period. But the *values* of the cost-of-goods-sold flow into the pump and the sales flow out of the pump are not the same: cost of goods sold represents the using-up of the boats at what they cost the company, but sales represents the delivering of the boats to customers at the price customers agree to pay for them. For example, if on Tuesday Pump & Paddle sells two boats, each of which cost it $18, at the planned selling price of $50, Tuesday's sales will be $100 ($50 per boat) and Tuesday's cost of goods sold will be $36 ($18 per boat).

The other $32 that is included in the sales value of each boat is additional value Pump & Paddle has put into the sales through other pipes that flow into the sales pump.

To achieve the first-year sales, Pump & Paddle will also have to use up some value received from suppliers and employees for selling, and some value for administration, like this:

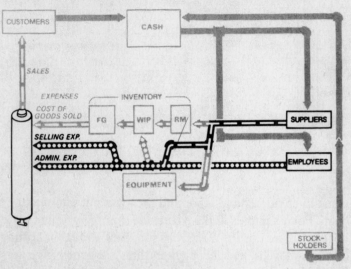

These two flows into the sales pump are the company's *selling expense* and *administrative expense*.

Each year as the company achieves sales it will also use up part of the equipment value it received earlier — see illustration at top of next page. This expense is called *depreciation*. It does not represent the departure of actual physical pieces of the equipment; it is the intangible loss of equipment value as the equipment ages and wears out and becomes obsolete, so it is shown as a dotted pipe.

The income statement back on page 1 shows that these four pipes flowing into the sales pump are all the expenses the company expects to have in its first year. They represent all the ways in which the company expects to use up value from suppliers and employees in achieving its sales over the year.

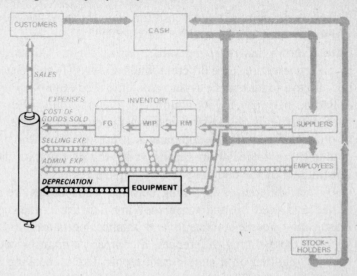

Since the company receives from suppliers and employees all the value it uses up in these expenses — rubber, production labor, selling and administrative work and supplies, and equipment — sooner or later the company has to pay cash to suppliers and employees for all this value used up as expenses:

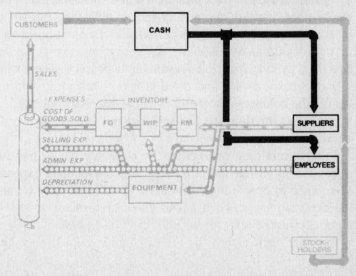

But *when* the company pays cash for these things is not necessarily the same as when they are used up as expenses. The picture shows that *receiving* value, *paying* for it, and *using it up as expenses* are three different kinds of flows — and they do not all have to take place at the same time. For example, Pump & Paddle may pay for its equipment a short while before or after receiving it. And after receiving the equipment value all at once at the start, the company will use up this value only gradually, as depreciation expense, with the part not yet used up still held by the company in its equipment tank.

In fact, differences in timing between when things are received and used up and when they are paid for is the basic reason that income statements and balance sheets are needed. Without these timing differences, a company's finances could be fully reported on a simple cash report, like a checking account statement. The company would own nothing but cash; and what it gains or loses over any period would be indicated by the difference between the period's cash inflows and cash outflows, and the resulting rise or fall in its cash level.

Basically, the reason for an income statement, which reports sales and expenses over a period, is that over the period of time the amount of value a company sells is different from what it receives payment for over the period, and the amounts of value that it uses up as expenses are different from what it pays for over the period. And the reason for a balance sheet, which reports what is owned and owed at end of period, is that, as a result, the company owns things it has received but not used up, is owed for things it has sold but not been paid for, and owes for things it has received but not yet paid for.

Still, at one time or another the company has to pay suppliers and employees cash for everything it uses up as expenses. So to keep from running out of cash, the company has to make the expenses for which it has to pay cash produce at least an equal amount of sales for which it can collect cash.

Say that each month the total of Pump & Paddle's selling,

administrative, and depreciation expenses were $12,800. Then, with each boat costing $18 to produce and selling for $50, to make sales value flowing out of the pump equal expense value flowing in, Pump & Paddle would have to sell 400 boats per month. Monthly cost of goods sold would be 400 boats times $18, which is $7,200. With the other three expenses adding up to $12,800 per month, total expenses flowing into the pump would be $20,000 per month. And monthly sales flowing out, 400 boats times $50 per boat, would also be $20,000 per month.

This would not necessarily mean that in any particular month the company receives and pays equal amounts of cash, because the company might collect cash for some of the month's sales in an earlier or later month, or might pay in an earlier or later month for some of what it used up as the month's expenses. But it would mean that each month's sales for which the company can sooner or later collect cash would equal the month's expenses used up for the sales that it has to sooner or later pay cash for. No profit, no loss.

Picturing the Income Statement

IF THE COMPANY can make the sales flowing out of the pump worth *more* to customers than the expenses that flow into the pump to achieve the sales, the company will make profit.

For example, say that each month the company can sell 500 boats at $50 each, instead of 400. Cost of goods sold will be 500 boats times $18, or $9,000. With the other three expenses totaling $12,800 per month, total expenses flowing into the pump will be $21,800 per month. But the resulting sales flowing out of the pump will be 500 boats times $50 per boat, or $25,000. So by using up as expenses each month a total of $21,800, the company will be delivering to customers sales value of $25,000.

The rest of the sales value delivered to customers each month, the other $3,200, will be called the company's profit before tax. In the financial picture, this value will flow into the sales pump near the bottom.

Government will maintain that *it* was indirectly responsible for *part* of this extra value flowing into the company's sales because it provided services that indirectly help the company, such as defense, police protection, and highways. Government will charge the company tax for these indirect services, and the company will have to pay government for the services. On the financial picture it looks like this:

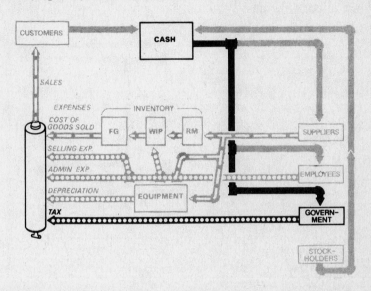

The dotted pipe from government to the sales pump represents the services that the government maintains it indirectly contributed to the company's sales. This flow is called *tax* because it represents these services at the value that government charges the company for them. And the solid pipe represents the company's payment of cash to government for the services.

On a company's financial reports for a year, what is meant by "tax" is what the company was charged in tax for that year, not the amount it paid for tax that year — as the picture shows.

For example, government may maintain that its services indirectly contributed half of the $3,200 in sales that did not come from expenses, in which case the amount of tax flowing into the pump will be $1,600 per month, and eventually the company will have to pay cash to government for the tax.

The *rest* of the value put into the sales, the part that does not enter the pump through expense and tax pipes — in this case the other $1,600 per month — comes from the company's own *value creation*, and is its *net profit* for the month. On the picture it looks like this:

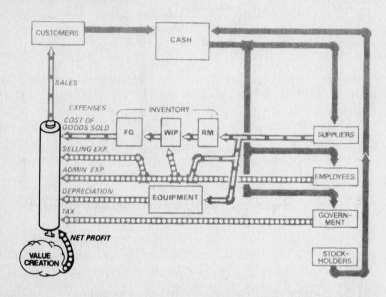

By using up $23,400 of value as expenses and tax for which it has to pay cash so well that it delivers $25,000 of sales value that customers will pay it for, the company has *created* $1,600 of value it delivered to customers as sales. That value created by the company is its net profit for the month.

As the picture shows, Pump & Paddle's net profit is not cash; it is a component of the sales value the company delivers to customers. However, Pump & Paddle does gain cash from its net profit: although Pump & Paddle does not have to pay anybody for its net profit, since it creates this value itself, it can collect cash for the net profit as part of the cash it collects from customers for all the sales value it delivers to them.

If the company does make net profit as planned, and as a result collects more cash for sales than it pays for value used up as expenses and tax, it may well pay some of this cash back to its stockholders as dividends:

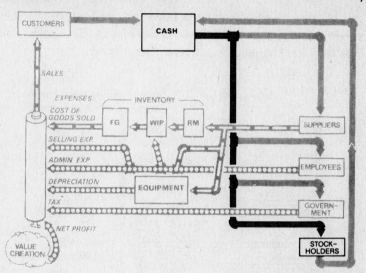

The dividends would provide return on the stockholders' earlier investment, which financed the company's start-up, and would probably improve the company's ability to attract more investor financing that it may need in the future.

However, the company is not legally obligated to pay the stockholders any dividends, or even to pay them back their original cash investment at any time. When stockholders invest in the company, they each get partial ownership of the company; this includes the right to vote in elections of the board of directors, who choose its president and vote on its biggest decisions, as well as the right to share any dividends the company may pay. But the stockholders do not get legal commitment from the company to pay dividends, or even to repay what they invested. The people they elect to run the company may decide that, instead of paying dividends, the company should use all or some of the cash it gains for other purposes that could lead to more net profit and dividends later — such as buying more modern equipment, designing a second product, or opening a West Coast sales office.

All of the company's planned flows into and out of the sales pump are now shown on the financial picture. These flows are exactly what the income statement reports on:

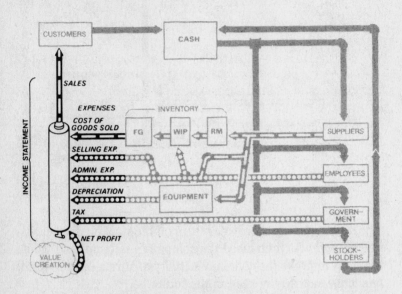

For comparison, here again is Pump & Paddle's predicted first-year income statement that the accountant prepared:

INCOME STATEMENT
First Year, in $000

Sales		$300
Expenses		
Cost of goods sold	$108	
Selling expense	75	
Administrative expense	60	
Depreciation	15	
		258
Profit before tax		$ 42
Tax		21
Net profit		$ 21

You can see that the income statement reports at the top the company's sales, which the picture shows represents value delivered to customers, from the pump; and below sales the income statement reports expenses, tax, and net profit, which the picture shows are the components of the sales, flowing into the pump.

Basically, the income statement is a report on how much net profit the company created over a period, and how. To calculate and explain the period's net profit, it reports the amounts of all the flows into and out of the sales pump over the period: sales value delivered to customers over the period, minus expenses and tax used up to deliver the sales, equals net profit that the company created and put into the sales.

· 4 ·

Picturing the Balance Sheet

To COMPLETE the financial picture of Pump & Paddle, we need to add symbols of one more type: meters, to keep track of what the company owes and is owed.

To represent these amounts-owed meters we will use ellipses. And to show how the amounts owed are determined by flows of value through the pipes already on the picture, we will draw wires to each meter from the pipes whose flows change its amount.

Think of each meter as working like the gas gauge in your car or the water meter for your house.

If some of Pump & Paddle's customers buy on credit, receiving boats first and not paying for them until later, then in the meantime Pump & Paddle will be owed money by these customers. The amount that the company is owed by its customers is called its *accounts receivable*.

On the financial picture, using our meter symbol, accounts receivable looks as shown in the illustration at top of next page. The ellipse is the meter that shows what Pump & Paddle is owed by its customers. The wire to this meter from the sales pipe, with a *plus sign* where it is connected to the meter, means that whenever some value flows through the sales pipe to customers the accounts-receivable meter reading *rises* by that amount — just as your car's fuel gauge rises when gasoline

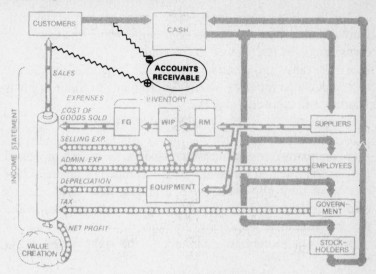

flows through the hose into your gas tank. For example, if on Tuesday Pump & Paddle delivers three boats to customers at a price of $50 each, accounts receivable rises by $150.

The second wire, which comes to the meter from the pipe for customer payment and has a *minus sign* where it is connected to the meter, indicates that whenever customers pay the company an amount of cash the accounts-receivable meter reading *drops* by that amount — just as your fuel gauge reading drops when gasoline flows from your gas tank into your engine. For example, if on Wednesday each of two customers pays Pump & Paddle $50 for a boat received earlier, Pump & Paddle's accounts receivable drops by $100.

The accounts-receivable meter keeps rising as Pump & Paddle delivers sales value to customers, and keeps dropping as customers pay the company, just as the picture shows. As a result, the meter's reading always indicates how much sales value the company has delivered to customers but has not yet been paid for — which is exactly what the company is owed by customers as of that moment.

This meter is located in the same center column as the company's tanks, because it too represents value the company owns: a pile of IOUs owed *to* the company.

All the tanks and meters in this center column of the picture represent the company's *assets:* the amounts of value it holds (tanks) and is owed (meters).

.

If the company owes amounts *to* outsiders, these amounts owed are also represented by meters on the company's financial picture, and they also have wires showing how each meter's amount is determined by flows through particular pipes in the picture. But meters showing amounts the company owes to outsiders are located in a column to the right of the assets column.

For example, if Pump & Paddle receives value from suppliers on credit, and does not pay for it until later, then in the meantime it will owe money to the suppliers. This amount owed is called *accounts payable*. On the financial picture accounts payable is represented by a meter like this:

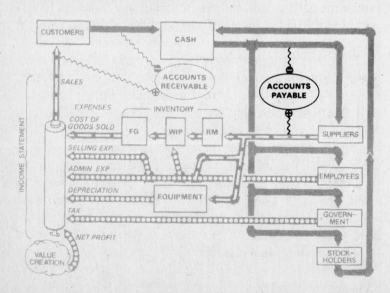

The wire to this meter from the pipe for inflows from suppliers, with a *plus sign* where it is connected to the meter, shows that when an amount of value comes in to Pump & Paddle from suppliers the company's accounts-payable meter reading rises by that amount. And the wire to the meter from the pipe for payments to suppliers, with a *minus sign,* shows that when Pump & Paddle pays an amount of cash to suppliers its accounts-payable meter reading drops by that amount. In other words, this meter works in the same general way as the accounts-receivable meter. It rises as supplies flow in and drops as supplies are paid for, and thus always shows how much has been received from suppliers but not yet paid for, which is exactly what Pump & Paddle owes to suppliers at that moment.

If Pump & Paddle owed money to other outsiders, such as employees or government, there would be other meters located in the same column as the accounts-payable meter. All these meters keeping track of what the company owes *to* outsiders represent the company's *liabilities.*

Another meter keeps track of what the company "sort of" owes to the stockholders who financed and own the company.

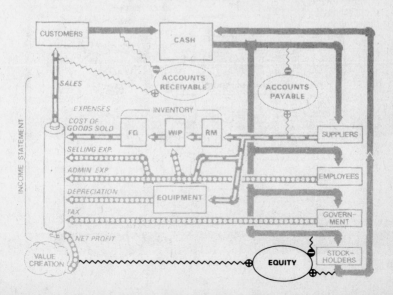

It is called *stockholders' equity* or simply *equity*. As the picture shows, this meter's reading rises when value flows through either of two pipes: it rises as stockholders provide cash to the company, and it also rises as the company makes net profit. It drops as the company pays cash back to the stockholders.

Thus, the amount of stockholders' equity represents how much the company has received from stockholders and made in net profit for them as its owners but has not yet paid back to them — what it sort-of owes to its stockholders.

This amount is not legally owed to the stockholders, in the way that liabilities are owed to other outsider groups; the stockholders are the company's owners, not its creditors. But stockholders' equity is a record of what the company would owe the stockholders, in just the way that the picture shows.

.

The financial picture now shows all the company's tanks and meters, and these are what the balance sheet reports on:

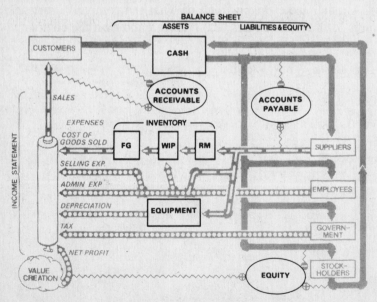

For comparison, here again is the predicted balance sheet that the accountant prepared for start and end of Pump & Paddle's first year:

BALANCE SHEET

Start and End of First Year, in $000

Assets	Start of Year	End of Year	Liabilities & Equity	Start of Year	End of Year
Cash	$ 50	$ 86	Accounts payable	$ 0	$ 0
Accounts receivable	0	0			
Inventory					
Finished goods	18	18			
Work in process	1	1			
Raw materials	6	6			
	$ 25	$ 25			
Equipment	75	60	Stockholders' equity	150	171
Total	$150	$171	Total	$150	$171

You can see that the balance sheet reports in one column the amounts of the company assets, that the picture shows are what it holds in tanks and is owed according to meters. And in a second column to the right of the assets the balance sheet reports the amounts of the company's liabilities and equity, which the picture shows are what it owes to others and sort-of owes to stockholders according to meters.

Basically the balance sheet is a report on how much value the company owns and owes as of a point in time, usually start or end of a business period. In one column are assets, what the company holds and is owed. And in the other column are liabilities it owes, and equity it sort-of owes to the stockholders who own it.

· 5 ·

The Whole Picture

THE FINANCIAL PICTURE of Pump & Paddle is now complete. The next page shows the complete picture.

A company's financial numbers are simply the amounts of value that flowed through the pipes in its picture, and the amounts left in its tanks and meter readings as a result of the flows. So to help explain the numbers we will enter them on the picture in subsequent chapters.

But first, in this chapter let's go over the picture to see how logically the report system reflects a company.

Look at the dashed pipes across the picture from suppliers on the right through the inventory tanks to the sales pump on the left, representing the company's production process. You can picture rubber flowing from suppliers to raw-materials inventory as the company purchases it; then flowing on to work in process, where the company adds labor value to turn the rubber into boats; then the completed boats moving on to finished-goods inventory, where they await sale; then, when they are sold, flowing out of finished-goods inventory as cost of goods sold. You can picture each inventory tank's level rising as value flows into it, and dropping as the value flows out and on.

Look, on the right, at the solid flows of cash that represent payments to suppliers, employees, and government. You can picture dollars flowing out from the company's cash tank

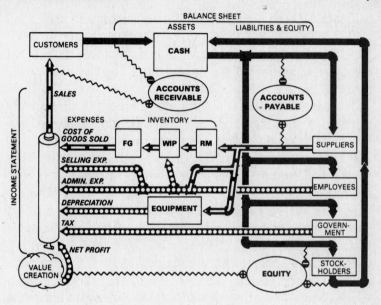

through these pipes to suppliers and others as Pump & Paddle pays for the value it receives from them and then uses up to deliver boat value to customers. And in the upper left you can picture dollars flowing into the company's cash tank through the solid pipe from customers as the company collects for the resulting sales. You can imagine the level in the company's cash tank dropping as it pays dollars out to suppliers and others, and rising as it collects cash from customers.

And you can imagine the meters keeping track of what the company owes and is owed as these flows occur: the accounts-payable meter reading rising as rubber flows in, and dropping back down as the company pays for it; and the accounts-receivable meter reading rising as sales flow to customers, and dropping back down as customers pay the company for the sales.

Basically, all financial reports are as logical and easy to understand as this picture indicates. Most businesses are more complicated than Pump & Paddle, and most companies' reports are fancier. And the *details* of accounting are highly complex. But fundamentally every company's reports reflect that company according to the same simple logic shown by the financial picture of Pump & Paddle.

What makes financial reports *seem* impossible to really understand is that they and their parts are almost always presented and explained separately, as bits and pieces, in a way that fails to show the logic that they all represent together. The key to understanding each report and each report part is to see how it fits into a logical complete picture of the business.

In fact, the very definition of each report and each report part lies in the picture's illustration of how it fits into the whole financial picture.

For example, consider the definition of cost of goods sold, reported on the income statement. From the financial picture, which depicts cost of goods sold and shows how it fits into the whole picture, you can define cost of goods sold as follows: Cost of goods sold is an amount of value that *flows* over a period. It represents some of the value the company used up for the period's sales by putting this value into the sales value the company delivered to customers over the period. Cost of goods sold flows from the company's finished-goods inventory, so it represents using-up of value that the company put into finished goods in making boats earlier, value that it got from suppliers and employees and has to pay them for. And since cost of goods sold flows from finished-goods inventory, it reduces the amount left in the company's finished-goods inventory, which is reported on the company's balance sheet.

By showing how each report and each report part fits into the entire picture, the financial picture itself provides you an excellent glossary of the reports and their parts, one that is much easier to understand and to remember than word definitions.

In addition to depicting all the parts of the two reports and showing how they are related, the financial picture of a business contains other elements that the balance sheet and income statement do not report. These include the outsiders that the company deals with, and the sales pump and value-creation symbols that help illustrate the income statement. None of these parts of the picture are either flows that represent actions of the company, or amounts of value owned and owed by the company as a result of its actions; they are "auxiliary" parts of the company's picture, representing some of the "places" it moves value from and to, and are shown in order to make the picture complete and understandable.

Much more important, the financial picture also shows all these *flows* of value which are not reported on the income statement or the balance sheet:

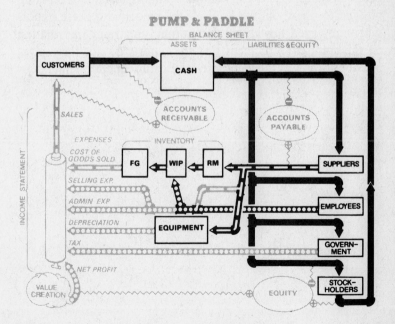

These unreported flows in the picture include all the inflows of value to the company's asset tanks, and all its inflows and outflows of cash.

You have to know about these unreported parts of the company's finances to make sense of the other parts that the two reports do specify. They show the company's receipt of and payment for the expenses and tax reported on the income statement, its collection for the sales reported on the income statement, and many of the inflows and outflows that determine all the levels reported on the balance sheet.

Furthermore, the amounts of these unreported flows are in themselves fully as important as the amounts of the other flows and levels that the balance sheet and income statement do report. Fortunately, once you know how all the reported and unreported parts of a company's finances fit together in its financial picture, you can use the numbers that the reports do provide to figure out for yourself the amounts of these important unreported flows, thereby gaining important information on the company's finances that the reports do not themselves provide — as we will demonstrate in subsequent chapters.

6

How Report Numbers
Reflect Company Actions

As NOTED early in the previous chapter, a company's financial numbers are the amounts of its flows and the amounts of its tank levels and meter readings as a result of the flows, so its financial numbers can be entered on its financial picture to help see what they mean.

To illustrate, let's enter Pump & Paddle's numbers on the company's financial picture to see how the accountant came up with the predicted numbers in the reports introduced in Chapter 1.

Here is the plan for starting the company that the Pump & Paddle founder-managers left with the accountant, after some discussion with him:

1. Boat-making equipment will cost $75,000, permit production of 6,000 boats per year, last five years or more.
2. Rubber will cost $12 per boat.
3. Manufacture of 6,000 boats per year will require three workers, each paid $12,000 per year.
4. Boats will be sold at $50 each.
5. Selling 6,000 boats per year at this price will probably require an advertising budget of $60,000 per year.
6. Management and staff should include the two founders, each

paid $17,000 per year, a sales manager paid $15,000 per year, an office worker paid $10,000 per year, and outside attorney and CPA services costing $6,000 per year.

7. The required building can be rented for $10,000 per year.

8. The accountant recommends that the company plan to keep on hand the following:

    a. Cash equivalent to two months' predicted receipts from customers.

    b. Finished boats equivalent to two months' predicted sales.

    c. Materials equivalent to one month's production usage.

    d. One thousand dollars' worth of boats in production.

    He predicts that tax will be 50 percent of profit-before-tax.

9. The equipment company agrees to permit free use of the equipment for a short period just before the company gets started so that the company can produce the inventory it wants to have on hand at start of first year. The workers agree to produce this inventory at a labor cost of $6 per boat produced.

10. At any time there may be a few customers owing money to the company, and the company may owe small amounts to materials suppliers, but the plan is to collect for all sales at time of sale and to pay for all purchases at time of purchase. All required financing will be raised from stockholders.

The accountant based the numbers in the predicted reports on this plan.

In the discussion, the two managers and the accountant agreed that the company would take three steps just before the start of the first year: raise money from stockholders, purchase and pay for the boat-making equipment, and purchase and pay for some rubber and labor and make some boats. By taking these three steps before the start of the first year, the company would be ready to begin selling boats as soon as the first year started.

Of course, before the company takes any steps, the amount

in each of its tanks will be zero, and the reading of each of its meters will be zero. Then each of its three steps will change the amounts of some of the tank levels and meter readings. The numbers that the accountant predicted for the company's balance sheet at start of first year represent his determination of what the company's tank and meter levels will be after the three steps.

So first let's use the financial picture to see how the three steps taken before the first year will change the company's tank levels and meter readings, from all zeroes up to the numbers the accountant predicted for start of first year.

The company's first step will be to get some cash from stockholders. The accountant figured that the amount the company should get from stockholders is $150,000, based on some calculations we will explain later. On the company's picture the numbers representing this action and its effects look like this:

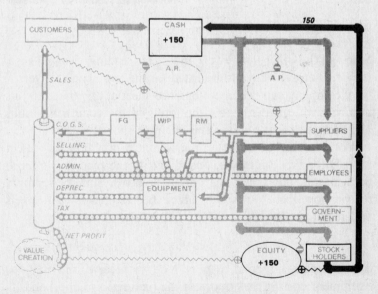

Each of these numbers represents value in thousands of dollars.

The cash inflow of $150,000 represents the company's action, and the rises of $150,000 in its cash-tank level and equity-meter reading represent effects of the action. The inflow of $150,000 goes to the company's cash tank, so it raises the level of the cash tank by $150,000, from zero up to $150,000. And because the equity meter is wired to pipes in such a way that its reading is raised by the amount of any inflow from stockholders, the company's equity meter reading also rises by $150,000, also from zero up to $150,000.

The numbers now on the picture show just how the first step will affect the company's balance sheet numbers. If the company prepared a balance sheet after just this first step, the balance sheet would report the company's tank levels and meter readings that are on the picture like this:

Assets		Liabilities & Equity	
Cash	$150,000	Stockholders' equity	$150,000
Total	$150,000	Total	$150,000

Since all the other tank levels and meter readings are still zero, they do not even have to be listed on the balance sheet yet.

A company can prepare a balance sheet at any time, and its numbers will always report the levels of the company's tanks and meters at that time, as this example shows.

You can see how *any* step the company may take will affect its balance sheet numbers. Just enter on the picture the numbers for the flows that the action involves, and then simply reason how these flows will affect the company's tank levels and meter readings.

·

The company's second step will be to receive and pay for equipment costing $75,000. On the picture this action and its effects looks like this:

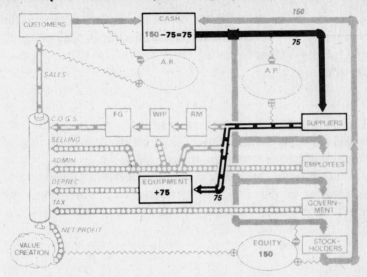

The action itself involves two flows: $75,000 of equipment value coming in from suppliers, and $75,000 of cash going out to pay for it. The inflow of equipment value goes from suppliers to the company's equipment tank, making the level of the equipment tank rise by $75,000, from zero up to $75,000. And the outflow of cash goes to suppliers from the company's cash tank, making the cash tank's level drop by $75,000, from $150,000 before the action down to $75,000 after the action. (The accounts-payable meter reading is raised $75,000 by the inflow of equipment, but is also reduced $75,000 by the cash outflow. Since both flows occur at the same time, this meter's reading stays at zero.)

If the company prepared another balance sheet right after this second step, it would look like this:

Assets		Liabilities & Equity	
Cash	$ 75,000		
Equipment	75,000	Stockholders' equity	$150,000
Total	$150,000	Total	$150,000

Again, as always, the balance sheet for this point reports the company's tank levels and meter readings as of that moment, and usually does not even list tanks and meters whose amounts are zero.

·

The company's third and final step before start of first year would involve several flows. The company would receive enough rubber and production labor to put the desired amounts of value into raw-materials, work-in-process, and finished-goods inventories. Here is how the flows and resulting inventory tank levels look on the picture:

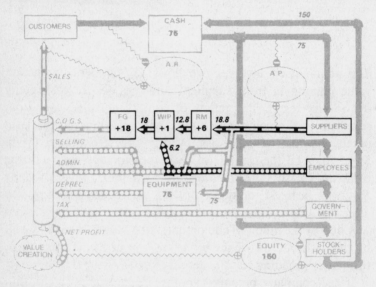

To understand them, it helps to start with finished-goods inventory and work backward.

According to the plan, the company wants to have in its finished-goods inventory enough boats for two months of planned sales; it plans to sell 6,000 boats per year, which is

500 per month, so a two-month supply would be 1,000 boats. And according to the plan each boat requires $12 of rubber and $6 of labor, a total of $18 of value put into each boat. So the company wants to put 1,000 boats, costing $18,000, into finished goods. This is why $18,000 of completed-boat value flows from work-in-process inventory to finished-goods inventory, raising the level of finished goods from zero to $18,000.

Again according to the plan, the company wants to have about $1,000 of partly made boats in its work-in-process inventory. The accountant estimated that on average each partly made boat would have half its production labor done, so each partly made boat would include $12 of rubber plus $3 of labor value and thus be 80 percent rubber and 20 percent labor. Therefore, the $1,000 in work-in-process inventory would include $800 worth of rubber and $200 of labor. The company has to move into work in process enough rubber to provide both the $12,000 of rubber in the completed boats that move on to finished goods, and the $800 of rubber in the partly made boats that remain in work in process; so $12,800 worth of rubber is moved into work in process from raw materials. And the company has to move into work in process enough labor value for the $6,000 in labor value in the completed boats that flow on to finished goods as well as the $200 in labor value in the partly made boats that remain in work in process; so $6,200 of labor value comes from employees into work in process.

In other words, the company moves into work-in-process inventory a total of $19,000 of value — $12,800 of rubber plus $6,200 of labor value. This provides just enough so that the planned $18,000 can flow on to finished goods, leaving the planned $1,000 in work in process.

According to the plan, the company wants to have in raw-materials inventory enough rubber for one month's boat production, which is one twelfth of the 6,000 boats to be produced annually, or 500 boats. Since each boat requires $12 worth of rubber, the desired amount of rubber in raw materials is $6,000. So the company has to move into raw-materials inventory, from suppliers, a total of $18,800 of rubber — enough for the $12,800 of rubber that moves on to work in process plus the $6,000 of rubber that stays in raw-materials inventory.

In total, the company puts $25,000 into inventory — $18,800 of rubber flows into raw materials from suppliers, and $6,200 of labor value flows into work in process from employees. These flows provide just the right amounts for the $25,000 of value the company wants in the inventory tanks: $18,000 in finished goods, $1,000 in work in process, and $6,000 in raw materials.

The company will pay cash for rubber and labor when they are received:

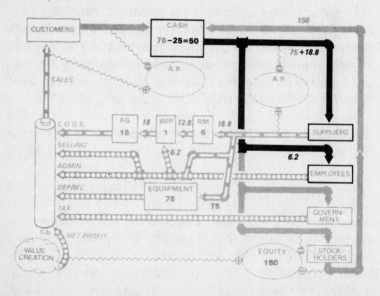

The company pays $18,800 to the suppliers for the rubber and $6,200 to employees for the production labor. These payments would take another $25,000 from the company's cash tank, reducing the cash level by that amount, from $75,000 down to $50,000. (Since these cash outflows to suppliers and employees equal the inflows of rubber and labor value from suppliers and employees, and occur at the same time, the company's liabilities would remain at zero.)

This cash level of $50,000 is just the amount that the company wants to have in its cash tank after completing the three steps. The company plans to sell to customers 6,000 boats per year, which is 500 boats per month, at a price of $50 per boat, so it plans to deliver $25,000 of sales value to customers each month and to collect the same amount of cash from customers each month. And according to the plan the company wants to have on hand an amount of cash equal to two months of predicted receipts from customers, so the amount of cash it wants to have is $50,000.

(The accountant calculated that the company should raise $150,000 from stockholders by figuring that it needed to raise enough cash to pay $75,000 to suppliers for the equipment, pay $25,000 to suppliers and employees for the rubber and labor for inventories, and still have the desired $50,000 left in the cash tank.)

After all three steps are completed, the balance sheet will again report the current tank levels and meter readings of the company, like this:

Assets			Liabilities & Equity	
Cash		$ 50,000		
Inventory				
Finished goods	$18,000			
Work in process	1,000			
Raw materials	6,000			
		25,000		
Equipment		75,000	Stockholders' equity	$150,000
Total		$150,000	Total	$150,000

These are exactly the numbers that the accountant's start-of-year balance sheet show.

.

From the picture you can see how logically the balance sheet numbers reflect what the company owns and owes as a result of its prior actions.

And you can use this understanding to reason out numbers you are not given. For example, if we were told only the amounts of the flows representing the three steps that the company planned to carry out before start of first year, and were not told the resulting balance sheet numbers, we could reason out for ourselves what the balance sheet numbers would be after the three steps are completed.

Or if we were given the start-of-year balance sheet after the company had taken the three steps, but were not told what the company had done, we could pretty well figure out the amounts of the unreported flows that produced the balance sheet levels and so learn what the company had done.

In either case, we would be using our knowledge of how the whole financial picture fits together to determine numbers we are *not* given from other numbers we *are* given and thus develop for ourselves a complete picture of the amounts of all the flows and levels.

7

How Report Numbers
Reflect a Company's Business
Over a Period

Now LET'S figure out the numbers for Pump & Paddle's planned first year. Let's say that Pump & Paddle has completed its first year exactly as planned, so the reports and numbers that the accountant prepared represent the company's actual reports for its first year.

The preceding chapter, showing how financial numbers reflect *individual* actions of a company, explained only the start-of-year balance sheet numbers. In this chapter, we shall see how financial numbers reflect *all* the actions of a company *over a business period,* through balance sheet numbers at start of period, income statement numbers for the period, and balance sheet numbers at end of period.

The best way to prove that you understand how the balance sheet and income statement numbers reflect a company's year is to figure out from them what happened to the company's cash over the year. Before reading on, turn back to the reports on pages 1 and 2 for a minute and see if you can determine from the report numbers the amounts of the company's cash inflows and outflows over the year, to explain why its cash level rose from $50,000 at start of year to $86,000 at end.

·

On a new copy of the financial picture for Pump & Paddle's first-year numbers, the company's tank levels and meter readings at start of year look like this:

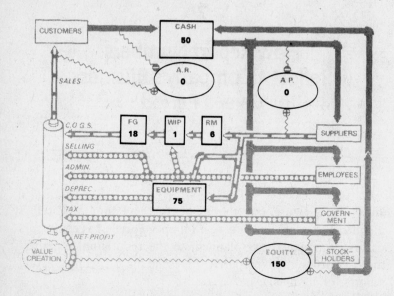

These are simply the numbers from the start-of-first-year balance sheet, which resulted from the three steps the company took before start of first year.

Next, the numbers that the reports specify for flows over the year can be entered on the picture, as shown in the upper illustration on the next page. These are the numbers that the first-year income statement gives us, specifying the amounts of the flows into and out of the sales pump over the year.

And now the numbers that the reports specify for tank and meter levels at end of year can be entered on the picture, as shown in the lower illustration on the next page. These are the tank-level and meter-reading numbers provided by the end-of-year balance sheet. On the picture, we have located them to

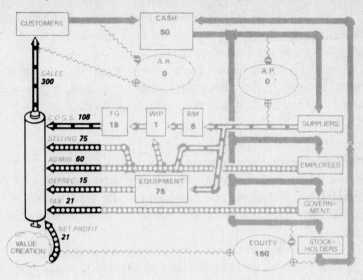

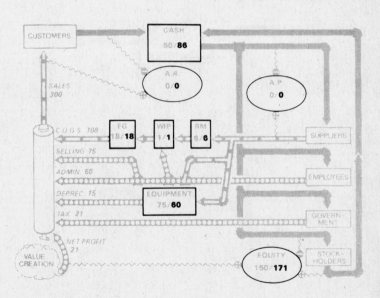

the right of the start-of-year numbers for the tanks and meters. For example, the 50/86 in the cash tank means that the cash level is $50,000 at start of year and $86,000 at end of year.

The picture now has all the first-year numbers from the reports. It helps to show what each reported number represents, and how they all fit together in reflecting the company.

Furthermore, on the picture we can now figure out the amounts of the *un*reported first-year flows. From these, we shall learn important information not provided on the reports and will be able to develop a complete picture of the company's first year.

For example, although it was not specified in the reports we can figure out the amount of cash that came in to the company from customers over the first year:

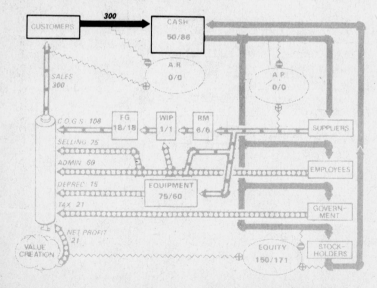

The income statement told us the sales flow was $300,000, and we know these sales caused accounts receivable to rise that amount. But the balance sheet told us that accounts receivable were zero at end of year, the same as at start of year. So we know that, to offset the $300,000 rise in accounts receivable caused by the sales, there must have been $300,000 of cash inflow from customers.

If the amount of cash received from customers over the year had been any less than $300,000, the end-of-year accounts-receivable level would have been higher than zero.

In a similar way, from knowing how all the financial parts fit together, we can figure out that the net amount of first-year cash flows between the company and its stockholders was zero:

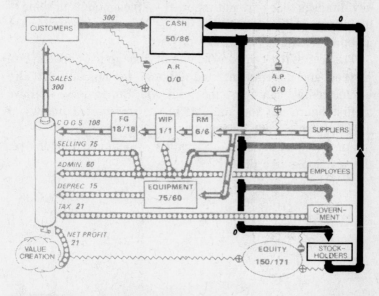

The income statement tells us the year's net profit flow was $21,000, and we know that this flow made equity rise by $21,000. And the balance sheet tells us that by end of year equity was exactly $21,000 higher than at start of year. So the net profit fully explains the change in the equity level. Since cash inflows from stockholders also increase equity, if such an inflow had occurred during the year the equity rise would have been more than $21,000. And since cash flows to stockholders decrease the equity level, if any cash had flowed to stock-

holders during the year equity would have risen less than
$21,000 or would have dropped. (It is possible that over the
year the company received some amount of cash from stockholders and paid the same amount of cash back to them, but
this would be an unusual coincidence, and we do not have any
evidence of it.)

.

By using our knowledge of the company's whole financial picture, we have now figured out from the report numbers some
key numbers that were not reported — the amounts of some of
its inflows and outflows of cash that helped to determine the
amount of cash it had at end of year.

The rest of the company's flows of cash go to suppliers, employees, and government, and although the amounts are also
unreported we can figure them out, too. But to do so we have
to first figure out the amounts of the unreported inflows of
noncash value from these outsiders.

For example, the amount of inflow of equipment value over
the year looks like this:

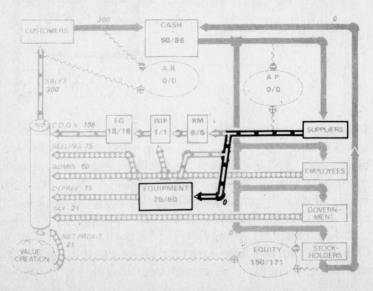

The income statement tells us that the year's depreciation was $15,000, and we know that this depreciation flowed out from the equipment tank. And the balance sheet tells us that the equipment level dropped from $75,000 at start of year to $60,000 at end, a drop of $15,000. The depreciation outflow is just enough to explain the change in the equipment tank level, so there could not have been any inflow to the tank. If some value had flowed into the tank, the drop in the equipment level would have been less than $15,000.

Here is what the year's unreported flows of rubber and production labor must have been:

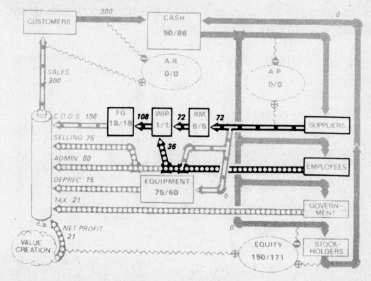

The income statement tells us cost of goods sold was $108,000, and we know this was an outflow from finished-goods inventory. And the balance sheet tells us the finished-goods inventory level was the same at end of year as at start. So over the year $108,000 worth of completed boats must have flowed into finished-goods inventory to replace what flowed out.

The balance sheet also tells us that the work-in-process level was the same at end of year as at start, so a total of $108,000 must have flowed into work in process to replace what left.

Since the outflow from work in process was completed boats, each two-thirds rubber and one-third labor, it's a good guess that the $108,000 flowing into work in process was $72,000 worth of rubber from raw materials and $36,000 worth of labor from employees. This would leave the rubber and labor percentages of work-in-process at end of year the same as at start, and there is no reason to believe they changed.

The balance sheet also tells us that the raw-materials inventory level was the same at end of year as at start. So $72,000 of rubber must have come into this tank from suppliers to replace the $72,000 of rubber that left.

The inflows of value related to the company's selling and administrative expenses look like this:

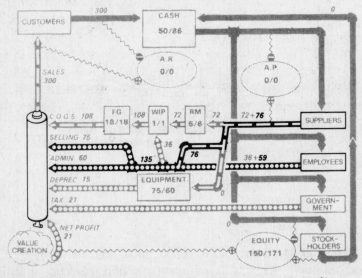

The income statement tells us the company used up $75,000 in selling expenses and $60,000 in administrative expenses, a total of $135,000. In order to determine how much of this total came from suppliers and how much from employees, to show the inflows from these two outsider groups on this picture, we had to go back to the plan. According to the plan, these expenses include $15,000 worth of work from the sales manager,

$10,000 from the office worker, and $34,000 from the two founder-managers, all of whom are employees; so employees provided $59,000 of work value included in these two expenses. The other $76,000 of what is used up in these expenses came from suppliers — outsiders who are not employees — including the advertising agency, the landlord, and the lawyer and the accountant. (If we did not have this information from the plan, we could still enter numbers for all flows on a complete financial picture of the company by sketching a separate tank on the right to represent all the selling and administrative suppliers and employees together, and showing a single pipe from this tank for the total $135,000 of value they all provide for the two expense categories.)

Now we have used our knowledge of the company's whole financial picture to figure out from the report numbers some more key unreported numbers: the amounts of physical and intangible value that the company received from suppliers and employees during the year.

With these amounts determined, we can now use the picture and the report numbers to figure out the rest of the company's cash flows, to suppliers, employees, and government:

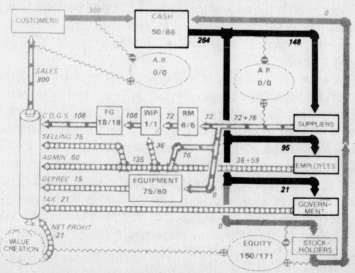

The balance sheet tells us the company had no liabilities at either start or end of year, so over the year the company must have paid each of these outsider groups an amount of cash just equal to the total value the company received from those outsiders over the year. Since we have now figured out what the company received from each outsider group, we know how much cash it paid to each: $148,000 to suppliers, for the $72,000 of rubber plus $76,000 for selling and administration received from them; $95,000 to employees, for the $36,000 of production labor plus $59,000 for selling and administration received from them; and $21,000 to government, for the $21,000 of tax value that the income statement reports was received and used up from government.

Thus, the total cash outflow over the year was $264,000 — to suppliers, $148,000; to employees, $95,000; and to government, $21,000.

.

Now we have a complete picture of *all* the company's financial numbers — not only the numbers for the year's flows reported on the income statement and for the starting and ending tank levels and meter readings reported on the balance sheet, but also the amounts of the unreported flows: the amounts received from outsiders, and the amounts of all the flows of cash.

One specific and very important advantage of knowing the unreported numbers is that we can now see and understand exactly why the company's cash level changed the amount it did from start to end of year. Over the year, the company received $300,000 of cash from customers, and paid out a total of $264,000 of cash to suppliers, employees, and government. It is these flows of cash, which put $36,000 more into the cash tank than they took out, that are the reason the company's cash level rises from $50,000 at start of year to $86,000 at end.

Obviously, these unreported numbers help make the reported numbers more understandable, by completing the picture and showing the amounts of the rest of the flows that are related to the reported flows and levels. In addition, these unreported numbers are just as important for us to know as those that were reported. In fact, the unreported numbers for the flows of cash are in some ways the most important of all the numbers: it is cash that the company must have to make required payments and avoid bankruptcy, to keep buying the things it needs to keep operating and stay competitive, and to pay return to the investors.

For these reasons, the kind of analysis of a company's numbers that we have applied to Pump & Paddle's first-year numbers in this chapter is *extremely* important in developing real understanding of any company from its report numbers. Later, we will provide more examples of the same kind of analysis. But if you are not sure you fully understand everything in this chapter, it would be a good idea to review it before reading on.

8

Cash and Noncash

IF THERE weren't any accountants in the world, and you and I were the founder-managers of Pump & Paddle, we would certainly develop and use our own reports on the cash parts of the company's financial picture:

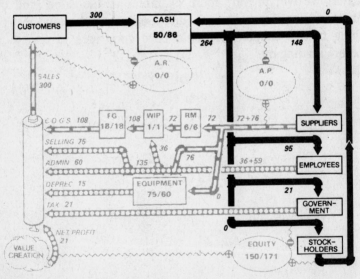

We would have no trouble preparing and understanding the company's cash report. For each period, the cash report would list the cash balance at start of period, the amounts of cash that came in from and went out to each outsider group during the period, and the resulting cash balance at end of period. The cash report for Pump & Paddle's first year would look about like this:

CASH REPORT

First Year, in $000

Cash at Start of Year		$ 50
Cash Receipts over Year		
From customers	$300	
From stockholders	0	
		300
Cash Payments over Year		
To suppliers		
Rubber	72	
Selling & administration	76	
To employees		
Production labor	36	
Selling & administration	59	
To government	21	
To stockholders	0	
		264
Cash at End of Year		$ 86

We could easily determine all these cash numbers ourselves — by counting the cash as it comes in and goes out, if we operate from our own cash box, or by maintaining the checkbook if we use a checking account. All the numbers would be simple facts, so to prepare and understand this report we wouldn't need an accountant or any accounting knowledge.

Despite the simplicity of the cash report, if we could have only one financial report on the company the cash report would be the best one to have — it would be more valuable than just the income statement, and more valuable than just the balance sheet. Ultimately, it is cash that the company needs to avoid bankruptcy, cash that it needs to buy what it requires to continue operating, and cash that it needs to pay return to those who have invested in the company. So to make sure it has and continues to have the capability to avoid bankruptcy, keep operating, and pay return to its investors, the most important thing for us to keep our eyes on is the amounts of cash it has, receives, and pays.

For the same reasons, a cash report is the most fundamental and valuable single report on *any* company, small or large. It is a shame that companies do not standardly provide cash reports along with their income statements and balance sheets.

But important as the cash report is, it is not in itself a complete financial report on a company, because every company also deals in value in noncash forms: physical goods, intangible value, IOUs. The very way in which almost every business gains cash is to trade cash for noncash items, then increase the value of these items, and then sell them to get more cash back. The Pump & Paddle financial picture shows this pattern. Pump & Paddle trades cash for noncash physical goods and intangibles such as rubber and labor, then turns these values into other noncash physical or intangible forms worth more to customers (boats) and sells them for more to get more cash back later. If in these trades the company receives before delivering or delivers before receiving, it will also have IOUs owed in and out.

So although a cash report is valuable, it does not report either the company's net gain in all value over a period, nor the company's net ownership in all value at start and end of a period. For example, over its first year Pump & Paddle will gain $36,000 in cash — but will also lose $15,000 in noncash equipment value, so its net gain in value over the year will be less than its cash gain, only $21,000. And at the end of the year it will have $86,000 in cash — but it will also have $85,000 in noncash value, inventory and equipment, so the total amount of value it owns will be more than its cash, $171,000.

The very idea of the income statement and the balance sheet is to provide reports on a company's gain and ownership in *all* forms of value, noncash as well as cash. The income statement reports on a company's gain over the period in all forms of value, net profit, by showing how much more noncash value the company sold and can collect cash for than it used up and has to pay cash for. And the balance sheet reports the company's ownership position in all forms of value, not only cash held but also noncash value held and value owed in and out.

In fact, the income statement and balance sheet are essentially reports on the company's noncash value. They report on the parts of a company's finances that a cash report would not report on. The balance sheet does report the company's cash level at start and end of period, but everything else reported on the balance sheet and income statement is noncash value.

To make the numbers for noncash values all comparable, so that they can be added and subtracted to figure out the total and net amounts of value a company gains and owns and owes, and so that numbers for different companies can be compared, all the noncash items as well as the cash items have to be measured in terms of the same unit of value. For example, if Pump & Paddle inventories were reported as 1,000 boats plus 30,000 pounds of rubber, you couldn't add these two figures to calculate a total inventory figure, or add these figures to the company's $50,000 of cash to calculate the total assets. And to make the universally used unit of value something that everybody understands, it has to be a unit of cash value — the dollar. If Pump & Paddle's inventories were reported as 1,000 boats plus 30,000 pounds of rubber, you wouldn't know how much *value* the inventories represent.

Thus, though most of the items reported on the income statement and balance sheet are not cash, they are all reported in terms of cash value — that is, in dollars of value. Pump & Paddle's finished-goods inventory is reported as 18,000 dollars of value, even though it is not 18,000 dollars but 1,000 boats. Raw-materials inventory is reported as 6,000 dollars of value, even though it is not 6,000 dollars but 30,000 pounds of rubber.

But the dollar values of noncash items are *not pure fact;* since the noncash items are not dollars, their dollar values *can-*

not be pure fact. For example, consider a boat in Pump & Paddle's finished-goods inventory. To make the boat, Pump & Paddle puts into it value costing $18, but the company will sell the boat for $50. When the boat is in finished-goods inventory, is it worth the $18 that it cost, or the $50 that it can be sold for? There is no single "true" answer to this question. To answer it, you have to *define what you mean* by the dollar number for a boat in finished-goods inventory: Do you mean what the boat cost, or what the boat will be sold for?

The rules that accountants use for determining the dollar numbers for the noncash items are called *generally accepted accounting principles*. The purpose of the principles is to make all companies' reports' numbers not only logical but also comparable, so all companies' reports are based on the same body of principles. But because companies do a tremendous number of different things, there are many principles for reporting on specific kinds of business activity, and the principles allow some flexibility so that each company's accountants can apply them in a way that they feel provides a fair picture of that company. To understand well any particular company's income statement and balance sheet numbers, it is important to read the notes that accompany the reports; they provide information on how accounting principles were applied to determine that company's noncash numbers.

•

But to understand *any* company's income statement and balance sheet numbers you have to understand the most fundamental of the accounting principles, because they affect the amounts and very meanings of the noncash numbers on every company's income statement and balance sheet. The principles that you have to understand are the basic rules accountants apply in order to answer two broad questions about the dollar values of the noncash items.

The first of these questions is: When do noncash things that a company sells for more cash than they cost become worth more than they cost? In other words, when does a company

make profit on things it sells for more than cost? On a boat
that Pump & Paddle first makes with things costing $18, and
later sells for $50, you could argue that it makes profit on the
boat when it *makes the boat* for less than the boat will sell for,
or when the company actually *sells* the boat for more than it
cost, or when the company actually *collects cash* for a boat
that cost less. Since in any year the numbers of boats a company makes, sells, and collects cash for may all be different,
the amount of profit for that year depends on whether profit
means gain from making products or gain from selling them or
gain from collecting for sale of them. And it is essential that
accountants use the same basic definition of profit in calculating it for all companies, so that readers of financial statements
such as you and I can learn what all profit numbers mean and
compare profit numbers of different companies.

The rule that all accountants use to answer this question,
and to calculate each company's profit for each year, is that a
company makes a profit on something when the company *sells*
it for more than cost. The financial picture with Pump &
Paddle's first-year numbers shows how this rule works:

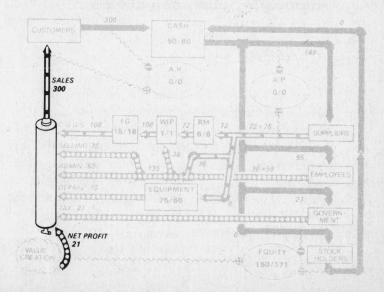

Net profit flows *into the sales pump,* as a *component of sales,* so net profit is made only when things are *sold* for more than the cost of what was used up to sell them. The only way that a company can make net profit is by actually selling things for more than cost, and the very *meaning* of net profit is the amount of value gained by selling things for more than cost. The picture also shows how this rule affects the amounts and meanings of numbers for expenses and assets:

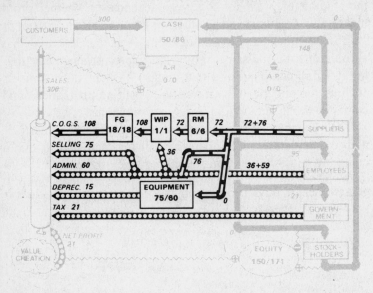

Until the noncash values that a company receives and then turns into sales enter the sales pump and *become* sales, all these values are reported as being worth only what they *cost.* In other words, all the numbers for noncash value on the way from outsiders on the right to the sales pump on the left reflect these noncash values at what they cost. For example, on the boat part of the Pump & Paddle picture, every number from receipt of rubber and labor, on the right, through the outflow of cost of goods sold, on the left, represents value at cost: rubber at $12 per boat, which it cost; labor at $6 per boat, which it cost; then boats at $18 each, which they cost.

Every balance sheet number for assets in tanks along the way, such as Pump & Paddle's inventories and equipment, reflects noncash value owned by the company at what it cost. And every income statement number for expenses and tax flowing into the sales pump reflects noncash value used up by the company at what it cost. Profit does not get added until this noncash value enters the sales pump and flows out as sales.

·

The second broad question is: When does a company use up value as expenses?

You could argue that value is used up as expenses when the company *buys* and receives noncash value, or when the company *pays cash* for it, or when the company *achieves sales* by using it. For example, does Pump & Paddle have $18 of expense when it buys rubber and labor for a boat, or when it pays cash for the rubber and labor, or when it sells the boat made from the rubber and labor? Since in a particular year the amounts of rubber and labor the company buys, pays for, and sells as boats may all differ, the amounts of expenses reported for each year depend on which meaning of expenses is applied. And since the amounts reported used up as expenses affect the amount reported as profit and the amounts reported remaining as assets, the profit and asset numbers also depend on how expense numbers are determined.

The most basic rule used to answer this second question and to determine the expense numbers is that a year's expenses are not the amounts of noncash value bought that year or paid for that year, they are the amounts of noncash value *used up to achieve that year's sales*. The financial picture shows the application of this rule in determining Pump & Paddle's expense related to rubber and labor:

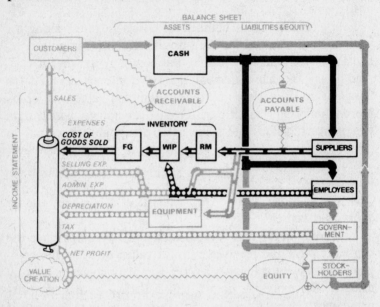

Expenses are noncash flows into the sales pump. Payments for rubber and labor are not expenses — they are entirely different flows, of cash to suppliers and employees, which may in any particular year be different amounts from what flows into the sales pump that year. Nor is the buying of rubber and labor the expense — receiving of rubber and labor is shown as inflows from outsiders to the company's inventory tanks, and in any particular year these inflows may also be different amounts from what flows into the sales pump as expenses that year. What *is* the year's expense related to rubber and labor, cost of goods sold, is the amount of rubber and labor value in the boats that are used up for that year's sales — that is, the cost of the boats sold that year.

Any rubber and labor value the company has bought but has not yet used up for sales is not reported as an expense flowing into the pump — it is reported as still being in the company's inventory asset tanks, still owned by the company and available for use in achieving sales in future periods.

The word "expense" does not mean an amount of noncash value bought, or an amount of cash paid for noncash value — it means an amount of noncash value *used up for sales*.

The same general approach is used to determine the amounts of other kinds of value used up as expenses each year, but for various kinds of value accountants use various methods for keeping track of what is used up as expenses and what is left as assets. For example, at Pump & Paddle, equipment value also flows into an asset tank when it is received, and then flows into the sales pump as an expense when it is used up for sales. But since the equipment is not what Pump & Paddle sells, as boats are, the accountants have to use another method for determining when equipment value is used up for sales. They figure that, since the equipment is expected to last five years, one fifth of its value will be used up for the sales of each of the five years it is used. So they report that one fifth of this equipment value, $15,000, is used up as first-year expenses for first-year sales; and at end of first year the company still has the other four fifths of the equipment value as assets that can be used up for sales in future years.

.

But at the end of any particular year it is not completely clear how much of the noncash value the company has used up for that year's sales and how much it still has at end of year for use in achieving future years' sales.

For Pump & Paddle equipment, it is completely clear how much the total depreciation expense will be over the total life of the equipment: by the end of the year in which the equip-ment stops working and becomes worthless, all of the $75,000 of value that has come into the equipment tank will have flowed into the sales pump as depreciation expense. But at the end of the first year the accountant cannot be sure how long the equipment will last. He estimated that it would last five years, and thus be used up one-fifth each year. But he could have estimated that it would last six years, and be used up one-sixth each year. If he had, he would have reported $12,500 used up as first-year depreciation expense. This would have resulted in his calculating and reporting a higher number for first-year profit, and also would have left $62,500 as the equipment asset value reported at end of year. When he prepares the first-year reports, though, he cannot know how long the equipment will last, so he cannot know which set of numbers to report for the first year.

If the accountant overestimates the amount of equipment used up as depreciation expense and underestimates the amount left as assets, the effect will be to make the first year's profit number lower and future years' profit numbers higher, because he will have subtracted more of the equipment's total depreciation expense to calculate the first year's profit, and will leave less to report as future depreciation and to subtract in calculating future years' profits. As a result, the first-year numbers he reports will tend to lead people to underestimate the company's financial health: they will see a lower profit number reported for the first year. Using this number as a basis, and not knowing that he has overestimated depreciation, they will be likely to anticipate relatively low profit in future years.

But if the accountant underestimates the amount of equipment value used up as first-year depreciation expense, and thus overestimates the amount left as assets, the effect will be to make the first year's net profit number higher and future years' profit numbers lower, because he will subtract less of the total equipment value to calculate the first year's profit and will leave more to subtract in calculating future years' profits. Consequently, the first-year numbers he reports will tend to lead people to overestimate the company's financial health: they will see a higher profit number reported for the first year; and, using this figure, and not knowing that he has underestimated depreciation, they will be likely to anticipate relatively high profit in future years.

In order to minimize the possibility that the numbers they report may lead people to overestimate a company's financial health, accountants will apply another general rule: where there is serious doubt as to how much of the noncash value has been used up and how much is left, lean the numbers toward understating rather than overstating a company's financial health, by reporting that the value has been used up as expenses rather than left as assets.

For example, if the Pump & Paddle accountant is not sure whether the equipment will last five years or six years, he would probably base his depreciation numbers on five years. He would report $15,000 of first-year depreciation rather than $12,500, thereby showing a lower first-year profit number and a lower amount left as assets.

Another example of this approach is the reporting of Pump & Paddle's selling and administration. The picture shows that when the company receives value to be used for selling and administration the value immediately flows across and into the sales pump as expenses, never stopping in an asset tank. It may well be that some of the selling and administration work that Pump & Paddle receives in its first year is planning work that will lead to sales in later years rather than the first year. But the accountant does not have any very reliable method for determining or even estimating how much of this value will help in achieving future years' sales, and thus could be called assets at end of first year, or for determining or estimating when it might contribute to which sales in future years. So he reports that all selling and administration value received in the first year was used up as expenses in the first year, and none remains as assets at end of year.

In almost every company's reports, the numbers reported as expenses are based in good part on accountants' judgment as to how much of the company's noncash value has been used up and how much is left. They have to be, because the accountants cannot know how much of the noncash value that the company has received will lead to future sales and thus has not been used up. When you review the notes accompanying the reports to see how accounting principles were used to determine the numbers, the most important thing to look for is how much the accountants may have overestimated or underestimated the amounts used up as expenses, and thus underestimated or overestimated the amounts made as net profit and left as assets.

If you find that the company has reported used up as expenses a good deal of value that you feel will probably lead to a lot of future sales, consider the possibility that it may have knowingly underreported its profit by a good deal and may be able to report considerably more profit in the future. But if you find a company has reported left as assets a good deal of value that you think may not help it achieve much sales and profit in the future, consider the possibility that the company has overstated its profit and may have to report much lower profit in the future.

Although the financial report system is superb at reflecting in a rational and succinct way almost everything that affects a company's finances, it does not reflect the effects of inflation at all well. The entire report system is based on the idea that the value of the dollar stays the same as the years pass. For any year, the more the value of the dollar has dropped over that year and recent years because of inflation, the more a company's actual financial progress and status differ from what its reports for that year indicate. Since inflation is now severe, and has been severe for several years, recent inflation now makes a company's finances significantly different from what its reports indicate.

By far the best solution to this situation — in fact the only good solution — is to stop the inflation.

In the meantime, the next best step would be to adjust the financial report system so that it does reflect the effects of inflation. However, the effects of inflation are so complex, and so difficult to understand, that there is not yet sufficient agreement as to the best way for companies to include inflation effects in their report numbers. So for the present financial reports are still prepared without including effects of inflation.

But larger companies are now providing, in one of the notes following their regular financial reports, some supplementary estimates of what certain of their report numbers would be if the numbers did reflect inflation. This information on estimated effects of inflation is fragmentary rather than comprehensive, and is not always presented or labeled as clearly as it could be. But it does give us insight as to how inflation makes three key aspects of a company's finances different from what its reports show, and this information is well worth looking at.

In a company's note on effects of inflation, these effects are calculated and presented in two different ways — one called *constant dollar* and the other called *current cost*. Accountants have not yet been able to agree which method is better, so they report both. The constant dollar method is the one that measures the effects of the decline in the value of the dollar, and that is what inflation is and why the inflation information is needed. So focus on the constant dollar method.

One of the three chief things you can obtain from a company's inflation note is a best estimate of what the company's net profit on its income statement would be if the report numbers reflected the effects of inflation. In the company's note on inflation there may be a table with a title indicating that its purpose is to show how inflation has affected the company's profit. In that table you can probably find a figure labeled as if it were net profit adjusted for inflation. Call this figure Number A.

In the same table you will probably also find a second figure labeled something like "gain from decline in purchasing power of net monetary assets," or "gain from decline in purchasing power of net amounts owed." Call this second figure Number B. This number represents the extent to which inflation has provided the company a gain by reducing the real value of the net amounts it owes — or if the number is a loss, by reducing the value of the net amounts the company is owed. In a very real sense this Number B is equivalent to an inflation-caused reduction in the company's effective interest expense.

Now, Number B should have been included in calculating Number A — because Number B is a gain due to inflation, and Number A is supposed to reflect the company's gain (net profit) including the effects of inflation. But the accountants do not include Number B in calculating Number A. So to obtain a best estimate of what the company's net value gain for the year was, add Numbers A and B. The result is the best estimate you can get of how much value the company really gained over the year, considering the effects of inflation. It is better than the net profit figure in the company's income statement.

(By the way, most current newspaper and magazine articles on how inflation affects profit fail to include consideration of the amounts that companies gain due to decline in real value of what they owe. As a result, these articles commonly include alarmist statements that due to inflation most companies' real profits are vastly lower than their reports show. These statements are *wrong*.)

Somewhere in the note on effects of inflation you may also find an item representing what the company's equity number would be if inflation effects were included. (In the inflation section some companies label this number "net assets" instead of equity.) This number is the best you can get as an indication of how much value from stockholders the company held at end of last year — that is, it is a better estimate of what the equity figure in the company's balance sheet is intended to represent.

And in the note on inflation you may also find a table designed to show what sales and a few of the company's other numbers would have been for each of the past five years if the effects of inflation were reflected in the numbers. This table is easy to understand, and it provides the best information you can get on how fast the company's finances are growing in real value.

·

In sum, expense and asset numbers represent the noncash values that a company uses up for sales at what they cost; the expense numbers for each year represent at cost the part of this value the company used up or may have used up for that year's sales, and asset numbers for end of each year represent at cost the rest of this value still there for achieving future sales. The profit number for each year represents value gained from that year's sales, calculated by subtracting from the year's sales the year's expense numbers representing what the company used up or may have used up for those sales.

The fact that these noncash numbers are not pure fact, but are based on rules that involve making estimates, means that to understand these numbers you have to understand these fundamental rules that help determine their amounts and their very meanings. But this does not make these noncash numbers any less valuable. To provide reports on the noncash parts of a company's finances, which you need in order to know about the company's whole financial picture, accountants *have* to use rules involving estimates. The rules they use are just about as reasonable and simple as the tremendous complexity and variety of businesses will permit. And, for those who understand them, the reports and numbers based on these rules represent superbly logical and concise information on companies.

· 9 ·

Profit and Cash

"IF WE MADE so much profit last year, why didn't our cash balance rise the same amount?"

For developing real understanding of financial reports and their numbers, this is the most important single question to ask and practice answering.

Cash and profit are the most vital parts of any company's financial reports. Cash is especially important because it is what the company ultimately needs to avoid bankruptcy, keep operating, and pay return to investors. Net profit is especially important because it measures the company's achievement of value gain, which will sooner or later show up as cash gain. And to understand and interpret net profit, and the rest of the income statement and balance sheet too, you have to be able to explain what they indicate about what happened to the company's cash. If you can't, you don't really understand the reports.

Yet the question above is probably what company presidents ask their accountants most frequently when they see their own companies' reports. What this means is that almost everybody needs help and practice in seeing how a company's profit and cash are related.

It is very common for a company to make a big net profit

over a year and yet end the year with less cash than it had at start of year. And a company that has a loss (negative profit) over a year will often end the year with more cash than it had at start of year. The amount that a company's cash rises over a year is almost never equal to its net profit for the year.

It is entirely logical that the amount of change in a company's cash level over a year differs from its net profit for the year. What determines the change in its cash level is all the inflows and outflows of cash over the year, but net profit is a single noncash flow.

Back in Chapter 7 we saw how the amounts of the flows of cash are related to the amount of net profit and the other noncash amounts in the reports. In that chapter, where we entered on the picture the numbers for Pump & Paddle's first year, we used the financial picture to figure out the unreported cash flow amounts from the noncash amounts the reports provided. Whenever you cannot explain the change in a company's cash level from the numbers on its reports, the most basic way to find the explanation is to use a financial picture just as we did in Chapter 7.

.

But once you understand the financial picture well, you can quickly find out directly from the reports why the change in cash level differed from the net profit. Just observe and interpret the changes in the noncash levels on the balance sheet.

Say that, after preparing for the first year as planned, over the first year Pump & Paddle collected cash for exactly what it sold, and bought and paid for exactly what it used up as expenses and tax, and had no dealings with investors. The company's balance sheet for start and end of first year would look like this:

BALANCE SHEET

Start and End of First Year, in $000

Assets	Start of Year	End of Year	Liabilities & Equity	Start of Year	End of Year
Cash	$ 50	$ 71	Accounts payable	$ 0	$ 0
Accounts receivable	0	0			
Inventory					
Finished goods	18	18			
Work in process	1	1			
Raw materials	6	6			
	$ 25	$ 25			
Equipment	75	75	Stockholders' equity	150	171
Total	$150	$171	Total	$150	$171

The levels of all the company's noncash assets and liabilities would all be the same at end of year as at start, because over the year the company received exactly what it used up, paid for exactly what it received, and collected for exactly what it delivered to customers. On its balance sheet only the equity and cash levels would change from start to end of year. Equity would be up by the amount of net profit — and the cash level would also be up by the amount of net profit, because cash collections would equal sales and cash payments would equal expenses and tax.

But in a typical year a typical business will receive an amount of cash larger or smaller than sales, from customers and perhaps investors, and pay an amount of cash larger or smaller than the year's expenses and tax, to suppliers, employees, government, and perhaps investors. This will make the rise in cash level larger or smaller than the year's net profit. It will also cause changes in levels of noncash assets or liabilities, or make the rise in equity larger or smaller than the year's net profit. So by noting these effects on the balance-sheet levels you can figure out why the change in cash level differed from the net profit.

To illustrate, consider Pump & Paddle's first year: net profit is $21,000, but the cash level rises $15,000 more — it rises by $36,000. The financial picture with all the first-year numbers shows why the cash-level rise exceeded the net profit:

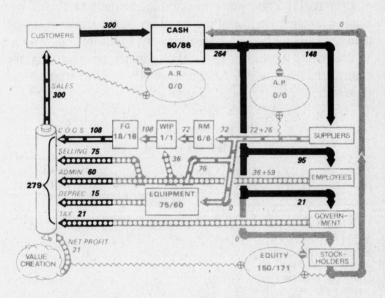

Over the year the company did collect cash for all sales, $300,000. But it did not pay out cash for as much as it used up in expenses and tax, which totaled $279,000 — it paid out only $264,000. It did receive and pay $72,000 for rubber and $36,000 for labor to replace the $108,000 worth of boats used up as cost of goods sold, and $76,000 to suppliers plus $59,000 to employees for the $135,000 used up in selling and administrative expenses, and $21,000 to government for the year's tax. But it did not in the first year receive and pay cash for the $15,000 of equipment value used up as depreciation during the year, because it had received and paid for this equipment value earlier. This is precisely why its total cash outflow was $15,000 less than the total of its expenses and tax, and that is why its cash level rose by $15,000 more than the amount of the year's net profit.

In other words, over the year the company collected cash for all of the $300,000 of sales, but over the year it did not pay for the $36,000 put into the sales as the $21,000 of net profit it created itself and the $15,000 of depreciation it had paid for earlier, so its cash level rose by $36,000.

You could spot this explanation simply by observing the changes in the noncash balance sheet levels from start to end of year:

BALANCE SHEET

Start and End of First Year, in $000

Assets	Start of Year	End of Year	Liabilities & Equity	Start of Year	End of Year
Cash	$ 50	$ 86	Accounts payable	$ 0	$ 0
Accounts receivable	0	0			
Inventory					
Finished goods	18	18			
Work in process	1	1			
Raw materials	6	6			
	$ 25	$ 25			
Equipment	75	60	Stockholders' equity	150	171
Total	$150	$171	Total	$150	$171

Compared to the preceding balance sheet numbers, for the situation in which the cash-level rise does equal net profit, the only thing different about how the noncash levels change is that the equipment level drops by $15,000, indicating that the company used up this much equipment value as expense without replacing and paying for it. All the other noncash assets and liabilities stayed unchanged, indicating that the company collected cash for all sales and paid for tax and for all expenses except depreciation. Equity rose by the amount of net profit, indicating that the company had no cash dealings with stockholders.

So the drop of $15,000 in equipment value on the balance sheet indicates why the cash level rose $15,000 more than the amount of net profit: over the year the company did not replace or pay for the $15,000 of equipment value put into the sales it delivered and collected for.

.

Another possibility is that in a particular year a company collects less in cash from customers than it delivers to them in sales, because it sells on credit. Say that in its first year Pump & Paddle operates exactly as planned, as shown in the picture and balance sheet just above, except that it has to permit customers to buy on credit in order to make its sales; and by the end of the year the company has collected cash for only $250,000 of its $300,000 of sales. Sales will still be $300,000, expenses still $258,000, and tax still $21,000, so net profit will still be $21,000. In terms of cash, total payments will still be $264,000, for all expenses except depreciation and for tax; but since cash receipts are only $250,000, the cash level will drop by $14,000 from start to end of year.

In other words, the change in cash level will be $35,000 less than the year's net profit — minus $14,000 compared to plus $21,000 — because, though the company pays $15,000 less than it uses up as expenses and tax, by not paying for depreciation paid for earlier, it also collects $50,000 less from customers than it sells due to extending customer credit.

In this case too, you can spot the explanation for the difference between cash-level rise and net profit by noting the changes in the noncash balance sheet levels from start to end of year:

BALANCE SHEET

Start and End of First Year, in $000

Assets	Start of Year	End of Year	Liabilities & Equity	Start of Year	End of Year
Cash	$ 50	$ 36	Accounts payable	$ 0	$ 0
Accounts receivable	0	50			
Inventory					
Finished goods	18	18			
Work in process	1	1			
Raw materials	6	6			
	$ 25	$ 25			
Equipment	75	60	Stockholders' equity	150	171
Total	$150	$171	Total	$150	$171

Here again the equipment level drops by $15,000, indicating that the equipment value used up as $15,000 of depreciation was not replaced and paid for. And in this case the accounts-receivable level also rises by $50,000, indicating that the company received $50,000 less in cash from customers than it delivered to them in sales. All the other noncash assets and liabilities are again unchanged from start to end of year, and the equity level again rises by the amount of net profit, indicating that the changes in the equipment and accounts-receivable levels reflect all the reasons for the difference between change in cash level and the amount of net profit.

In sum, the drop of $15,000 in the equipment level indicates that over the year the company did not replace and pay for $15,000 of depreciation expense, and the rise of $50,000 in accounts receivable indicates that over the year it collected $50,000 less than sales; so by examining the balance sheet you can explain why the change in cash level was $35,000 less than net profit.

There are many other ways in which a company's cash receipts and payments can differ from its sales and expenses and tax, causing differences between cash-level change and net profit. For example, in a later year Pump & Paddle may collect more cash from customers than it delivers in sales that year, by collecting for some prior-year sales; or buy and pay for more rubber than it uses up in expenses that year; or pay suppliers less than the amount of value it receives from them and uses up; or borrow cash from a bank; or pay dividends to stockholders. But whatever a company does, the reasons for the resulting difference between the change in its cash level and the net profit will be clear on its financial picture.

And you can find the reasons by noting the changes in the company's noncash balance sheet levels over the year. If it collects more cash from customers than it sells that year, you can find this out by spotting the drop in its accounts-receivable level. If it buys and pays for more rubber than it uses up, you can find this out by spotting the rise in inventory level. If it pays suppliers for less than it receives from them, you can find this out by spotting the rise in accounts payable. If it pays dividends to stockholders, you can find this out by spotting the fact that equity rises that much less than net profit.

Other things being equal, a rise in any noncash asset means the cash level rose that much less than net profit: if accounts receivable rose, the company collected from customers that much less than it sold to them; and if some other asset rose, the company received and paid for that much more than it used up as expenses. Correspondingly, a drop in a noncash asset means the rise in cash level was that much more than net profit: the company collected that much more than it sold, or received and paid for that much less than it used up as expenses. In other words, of all its asset value, the more that is in noncash forms the less is in cash.

Other things being equal, a rise in any liability means the cash level rose that much more than net profit, because it means the company paid for that much less than it received and used up, or borrowed that much cash; correspondingly, a drop in a liability level means the cash level rose that much less than net profit. In other words, everything else being equal, the more it has received on credit the more cash it has.

And, other things being equal, if the equity level rises less than the amount of net profit, the cash-level rise will be that much less than net profit, and vice versa, because it indicates that the company paid that much in dividends or received that much cash from stockholders.

Why don't companies give us their whole financial picture with all the numbers, instead of just the income statement and the balance sheet? Or at least provide us the cash report along with the other two so that we don't have to figure out the critically important cash flow amounts for ourselves?

Toward the objective of reporting to us on the parts of companies' financial pictures that their income statements and balance sheets do not report, most companies' accountants now provide a third report called the *statement of changes in financial position*.

Sometimes this report is exactly the cash report — just what is needed to complete the picture that the income statement and the balance sheet describe in part, and just what is needed to provide information on the flows of cash that are so important to the company and its investors.

But unfortunately this third report is usually presented in a slightly different format that makes it vastly more difficult to understand and relate to the financial picture.

It is usually presented as a report on *net working capital* rather than on cash. Net working capital is the amount by which a company's *current assets* exceed its *current liabilities*. Current assets means cash plus those other assets likely to be traded for cash within the next year, such as Pump & Paddle's cash, accounts receivable, and inventories. And current liabilities means those likely to be paid off with cash within the next year, such as Pump & Paddle's accounts payable if it had any. At Pump & Paddle, net working capital would be cash plus accounts receivable plus inventories minus accounts payable — $75,000 at start of year, and $111,000 at end of year.

The amount of a company's net working capital has meaning, related to its cash: it represents the amount of cash the company would have left if it traded all its current assets for cash, without profit, and paid off all its current liabilities with cash. But in our financial picture you can't see net working capital flowing in and out, because it isn't exactly any of the things that flow through the picture's pipes. It isn't exactly cash, or exactly physical goods such as rubber and boats, or exactly intangible value such as labor — or even exactly amounts owed. It is essentially just numbers, arrived at by adding and subtracting all of these things.

We could come up with a financial picture that shows net working capital flowing in and out, but to do so we would have to change our financial picture so much that it would no longer depict and explain all the individual parts that the income statement and balance sheet report on, or even show clearly all the flows of cash. And in addition this revised picture of net working capital would be too abstract for most of us to understand. To see what I mean, try to imagine that what is flowing through a pipe is "differences between (a) amounts of cash and accounts receivable and three kinds of inventory and (b) amounts of accounts payable."

In other words, a third report on net working capital does not report to us on the rest of our financial picture, which is what we need and what a cash report would do perfectly. Instead, it reports on the company according to a different and much less comprehensible picture. To retain what our picture now has, and to avoid confusing abstractions, we will keep the picture we have.

Another confusing aspect of reports on net working capital is that they often describe some of the causes of changes in the net-working-capital level obliquely, not directly. Instead of explaining the rise or fall by listing the inflows and outflows that were its cause, the report will usually list some of these flows; but in place of the rest it will list changes in other balance sheet levels that these flows also caused. For example, an inflow of cash from a bank providing a five-year loan would increase a company's net working capital; but instead of reporting this inflow of cash as the cause of the rise, the report will list the rise in debt that the flow also causes. To an expert this may seem a silly complaint — but to the layman trying to understand the report this kind of thing is murder.

If a company's third report is presented in terms of net working capital instead of cash, figure out for yourself as well as you can what happened to the company's cash over the year, using the techniques described in Chapter 7 and earlier in this chapter. By doing so, you will obtain all the information that the net-working-capital report is intended to provide, but in a format that fits and completes your financial picture of the company and is vastly easier to grasp than the net-working-capital report.

Picturing Any Company

MOST OTHER COMPANIES have financial reports that include terms at least a little different from those on the Pump & Paddle reports, and some other companies' reports look quite different from those of Pump & Paddle. But every company's reports reflect a financial picture of what that company does, owns, and owes. Each company's financial picture is based on the same fundamental logic as Pump & Paddle's picture and is basically just as complete as Pump & Paddle's. And most other companies' complete financial pictures look quite similar to Pump & Paddle's picture.

So by starting with the financial picture of Pump & Paddle you can sketch a financial picture of any company and then use it to understand that company's reports and numbers.

·

One way in which the reports of various companies are dissimilar is in use of different words to label the same things. For example, sales are sometimes called revenues or income. Cost of goods sold is sometimes called cost of sales. Profit is very often called income and sometimes called earnings. (Watch out for the word "income." Since it is often used in place of the word "profit," and sometimes in place of "sales" or "revenue," you have to look carefully to see which of these flows it represents.) Stockholders' equity is sometimes called net worth or capital.

To make the Pump & Paddle financial picture suitable for another company that uses different terms for the same things, you don't need to change any pipes or tanks or meters. Just relabel the appropriate ones to show which parts of the picture each term on that company's reports represents.

If the company you are interested in does different things from what Pump & Paddle does, the pipes and tanks and meters in its picture will not be exactly the same as those in the Pump & Paddle picture, but they will represent the other company's actions and their effects just as logically. To illustrate, let's consider how Pump & Paddle's picture would be changed if Pump & Paddle did different things from what it plans to do.

Say that the company is a boat retailer instead of a boat manufacturer. The part of its picture representing its getting and owning of boat value would probably be changed to look like this:

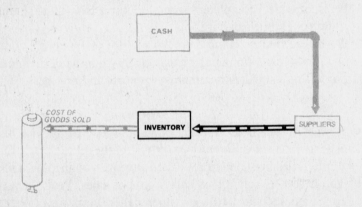

The company simply receives completed boats from a supplier and keeps them in a single inventory tank until sale. Its picture would have neither a raw-materials inventory tank for rubber to make boats with nor a work-in-process tank representing the boats it is making; it would have a single inventory tank for completed boats received but not yet sold. And the value it receives and pays for in getting its boats does not include rubber from suppliers and production labor from employees. The value is simply completed boats coming in from a supplier who makes or wholesales the boats.

The company's reports would be a reflection of its financial picture, so the inventory section would be changed like this:

INCOME STATEMENT

Sales		$ xx
Expenses		
Cost of goods sold	$ xx	
Selling expense	xx	
Administrative expense	xx	
Depreciation	xx	
		xx
Profit before tax		$ xx
Tax		xx
Net profit		$ xx

BALANCE SHEET

Assets		Liabilities & Equity	
Cash	$ xx	Accounts payable	$ xx
Accounts receivable	xx		
Inventory	XX		
Finished goods	xx		
Work in process	xx		
Raw materials	xx		
	$ xx		
Equipment	xx	Stockholders' equity	xx
Total	$ xx	Total	$ xx

These reports do not show all the parts of the company's finances and how they fit together; for example, the reports do not show that there is no flow of value from employees into inventory. But they reflect the company's financial picture, which does show these things.

.

If Pump & Paddle sold services instead of products to its customers, by providing instruction in boating to people who already own boats, the part of its picture that replaces making and selling boats might look like this:

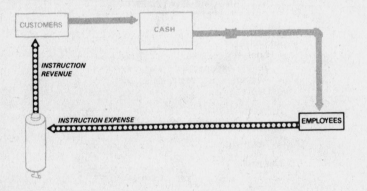

Each day as the instructors work for the company this work is received and flows right out as that day's instruction expense, never stopping in an asset tank, as the original Pump & Paddle's selling and administration work did. And whatever instruction the company delivers to customers that day, measured in terms of what they agree to pay for it, flows to the customers, as boat sales did; but it is a dotted intangible flow, a service delivered to customers, and might be labeled instruction revenue.

Compared with the items on the reports we have been looking at, the elements listed on the company's reports would look like this:

INCOME STATEMENT

Instruction revenue
~~Sales~~ $ xx

Expenses
  Instruction expense
  ~~Cost of goods sold~~ $ xx
  Selling expense   xx
  Administrative expense   xx
  Depreciation   xx
                            xx

Profit before tax $ xx
  Tax   xx
Net profit $ xx

BALANCE SHEET

Assets		Liabilities & Equity	
Cash	$ xx	Accounts payable	$ xx
Accounts receivable	xx		
Inventory			
Finished goods	xx		
Work in process	xx		
Raw materials	xx		
	$ xx		
Equipment	xx	Stockholders' equity	xx
Total	$ xx	Total	$ xx

The reports do not show that revenue represents value the company delivers to its customers; but they reflect the company's financial picture, which does show this.

Another company providing services to customers might report its receipt of service work from its employees as flowing into an inventory-like asset tank, and then flowing to the sales pump as expenses. For example, if, instead of providing instruction services on boating, Pump & Paddle conducted studies on public interest in boating on contract to state parks plan-

ning new boating facilities, the part of its picture representing
its receipt and use of employee work on the studies might look
like this:

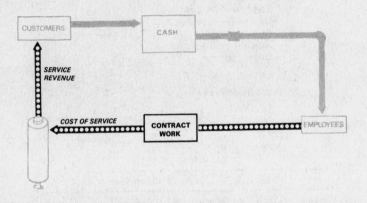

Once a contract is made to carry out a study, then work being
done on that study by employees flows into an asset tank. When
the study is completed this value flows into the sales pump as
expenses and its delivery to the customers is reported as sales.

In this case, the elements on the company's reports would
differ from those on Pump & Paddle's original reports in this
way:

INCOME STATEMENT

Service revenue ~~Sales~~		$ xx
Expenses **services**		
Cost of ~~goods sold~~	$ xx	
Selling expense	xx	
Administrative expense	xx	
Depreciation	xx	
		xx
Profit before tax		$ xx
Tax		xx
Net profit		$ xx

BALANCE SHEET

Assets		Liabilities & Equity	
Cash	$ xx	Accounts payable	$ xx
Accounts receivable	xx		
Contract work	XX		
~~Inventory~~			
~~Finished goods~~	~~xx~~		
~~Work in process~~	xx		
~~Raw materials~~	xx		
	$ xx		
Equipment	xx	Stockholders' equity	xx
Total	$ xx	Total	$ xx

The preceding two pictures represent two different approaches for a service company's deciding when to report as expenses the employees' work on the services. The difference between the two is a good example of the kind of thing to look for when reading the notes to a company's reports to see how the accountants applied accounting principles to determine the expenses. Two companies in very similar service businesses may use different methods for determining their expenses used up and assets remaining — one reporting employee work on the services used up as soon as received, and the other reporting only part of the work used up and the rest still there as assets. Each company's accountants probably have a very good defense for the method they used, so neither company's report numbers are "wrong" — but relatively speaking the first company's numbers are more likely to be understating its financial health, and the second company's numbers are more likely to be overstating its financial health. So everything you can spot about this difference in accounting methods will help you in comparing the two companies' finances.

•

If Pump & Paddle bought and then gradually used up office furniture as well as production equipment, just above the parts representing equipment its picture might have additional parts like this:

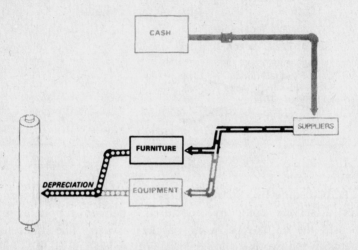

As furniture is received, it flows into an additional asset tank labeled office furniture. As this furniture is used and gradually loses value, depreciation flows out from this tank, entering the sales pump as part of a single expense representing depreciation of both furniture and equipment.

In this situation, the elements listed in the company's reports would differ from those on the original reports like this:

INCOME STATEMENT

Sales		$ xx
Expenses		
Cost of goods sold	$ xx	
Selling expense	xx	
Administrative expense	xx	
Depreciation	xx	
		xx
Profit before tax		$ xx
Tax		xx
Net profit		$ xx

BALANCE SHEET

Assets		Liabilities & Equity	
Cash	$ xx	Accounts payable	$ xx
Accounts receivable	xx		
Inventory			
Finished goods	xx		
Work in process	xx		
Raw materials	xx		
	$ xx		
Furniture	XX		
Equipment	xx	Stockholders' equity	xx
Total	$ xx	Total	$ xx

The reports do not report the inflow of furniture or the outflow of cash to pay for it. Nor do they specifically show that furniture and equipment depreciation joined and flowed into the pump together. But the reports are a reflection of the company's financial picture, where these things are shown.

If Pump & Paddle did not pay its employees until a while after receiving work from them, its financial picture would have another meter something like this:

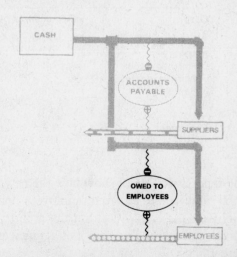

This meter would keep track of what the company owes to its employees, in the same way as the accounts-payable meter keeps track of what it owes to its suppliers: its reading rises as value flows in from employees, and drops as the company pays the employees for the work.

In this case, the things listed on the company's reports would differ from those on the original reports like this:

INCOME STATEMENT

Sales		$ xx
Expenses		
Cost of goods sold	$ xx	
Selling expense	xx	
Administrative expense	xx	
Depreciation	xx	
		xx
Profit before tax		$ xx
Tax		xx
Net profit		$ xx

BALANCE SHEET

Assets		Liabilities & Equity	
Cash	$ xx	Accounts payable	$ xx
Accounts receivable	xx	**Owed to employees**	**XX**
Inventory			
Finished goods	xx		
Work in process	xx		
Raw materials	xx		
	$ xx		
Equipment	xx	Stockholders' equity	xx
Total	$ xx	Total	$ xx

The reports would not show how the new meter's level rises as work-value comes in from employees and drops as the company pays the employees; but the reports are a reflection of a logical picture of the company's finances, which does show these things.

If Pump & Paddle paid suppliers before receiving value from them, instead of afterward, then instead of an accounts-payable meter the company's financial picture would have another meter:

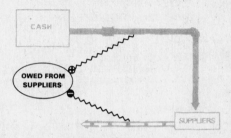

The meter keeping track of what is owed from dealings with suppliers is located in Pump & Paddle's *assets* column, rather than its liabilities column, because it represents how much Pump & Paddle *is owed by* suppliers as a result of the company's paying early, instead of how much Pump & Paddle owes to suppliers as a result of its paying late. The amount that the company is owed by its suppliers rises when it pays them in advance; it drops when the suppliers later deliver things already paid for.

If this were the situation at Pump & Paddle, the elements listed on its reports would differ from those on the original reports like this:

INCOME STATEMENT

Sales		$ xx
Expenses		
Cost of goods sold	$ xx	
Selling expense	xx	
Administrative expense	xx	
Depreciation	xx	
		xx
Profit before tax		$ xx
Tax		xx
Net profit		$ xx

(*reports continued at top of next page*)

BALANCE SHEET

Assets		Liabilities & Equity	
Cash	$ xx	Accounts payable	$ xx
Accounts receivable	xx		
Owed from suppliers	XX		
Inventory			
Finished goods	xx		
Work in process	xx		
Raw materials	xx		
	$ xx		
Equipment	xx	Stockholders' equity	xx
Total	$ xx	Total	$ xx

The reports would not show that the new asset is a meter whose
reading rises as the company pays suppliers in advance and
drops as they deliver goods or services later, but they reflect
the financial picture of the company where we can see these
things.

For the meters in each of the two preceding pictures, representing respectively what the company owes to employees and
what it is owed by suppliers, the pictures show these meters
labeled in laymen's language indicating what each represents.
But for either of these two meters the accountants might use a
label that is terribly confusing to people like us: the amount
owed to employees might be reported as *accrued expenses,* and
the amount owed from suppliers might be called *prepaid expenses.* The problem with these labels is that neither of the
items is an expense. As you know, an expense is a flow to the
sales pump of value used up over a period, reported on the income statement; but these items are amounts owed, out and
in at end of period, one a liability and the other an asset, and
both are reported on the balance sheet.

Whenever you see any term including the word "expenses"
reported on a balance sheet, it is not an expense — it is a
poorly labeled asset if it is in the assets column, or a poorly

labeled liability if it is in the liabilities column. A balance sheet always reports only assets, liabilities, and equity — not expenses.

.

If Pump & Paddle received some of its investor financing from lenders, rather than all from stockholders, the parts of the financial picture depicting its dealings with lenders would look like this:

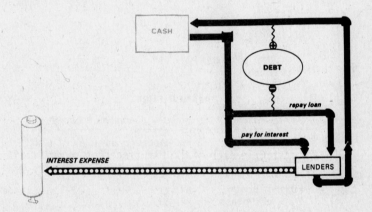

First, cash comes in from lenders, at far right. In letting the company keep this borrowed money as time passes, the lenders are providing Pump & Paddle additional value for which they charge interest: the right to hold the money, an intangible value that Pump & Paddle gradually receives and uses up as interest expense. The company pays the lenders cash for the interest, and later pays them back the cash they lent. And a Pump & Paddle liability meter labeled debt keeps track of the amount the company has borrowed but not yet paid back. (If the company delayed its payments for interest, there would be another liability meter keeping track of what the company owes for interest.)

If this were the situation, the company would list these items on its reports:

INCOME STATEMENT

Sales		$ xx
Expenses		
Cost of goods sold	$ xx	
Selling expense	xx	
Administrative expense	xx	
Depreciation	xx	
Interest	XX	
		xx
Profit before tax		$ xx
Tax		xx
Net profit		$ xx

BALANCE SHEET

Assets		Liabilities & Equity	
Cash	$ xx	Accounts payable	$ xx
Accounts receivable	xx		
Inventory			
Finished goods	xx		
Work in process	xx		
Raw materials	xx		
	$ xx	Debt	XX
Equipment	xx	Stockholders' equity	xx
Total	$ xx	Total	$ xx

The reports would not show the flows of cash from and to lenders, which are the basic causes of these report additions, nor would they show that the debt liability is a meter whose level rises when borrowed cash is received and drops as it is paid back. But the reports reflect a financial picture that does show these things.

There are many other ways in which Pump & Paddle or a company you are interested in may do things differently from what Pump & Paddle does in its original plan, and many other things a company may own and owe as a result. But whatever a company does and owns and owes as a result, its financial reports are reflections of a very logical and integrated complete financial picture of that company's flows and resulting possessions and debts.

By studying any company's financial reports and thinking about what it does, you can turn the original picture of Pump & Paddle into a picture of that particular company as its reports reflect it. And by doing so you can develop a clear understanding of how each and all the report parts reflect that company, and figure out what the numbers say about its actions and resulting status, in the same way that we have done for the original Pump & Paddle.

· 11 ·

Ratios, for Comparisons and Insights

A FINANCIAL RATIO for a company is one of the company's financial numbers divided by another of the company's numbers, to express the first number as a fraction or percentage of the second.

For example, for Pump & Paddle, one financial ratio is the company's first-year net profit of $21,000 divided by the company's start-of-year equity of $150,000. This ratio equals 7/50 or 14 percent, indicating that first-year net profit is 14 percent of start-of-year equity.

This particular ratio, annual net profit divided by equity, is called the *return-on-equity* ratio, or simply return on equity. It measures net profit as a percentage of the stockholder financing employed to achieve the profit, in the same way that an interest rate measures interest on a bank account as a percentage of the amount deposited in the bank to earn the interest.

In many books and courses on finance and accounting, and in much of the financial community, the calculation of financial ratios for a company is treated as if it were the great key to understanding and analyzing the company's finances. Financial ratios are not this important at all. The key to understanding a company's finances, as we have discussed, is seeing how all the reports and their elements and numbers fit together as a picture of the company's finances. And the key to analyzing a company's finances is using this understanding to predict what the company's finances may be in the future, and to measure its anticipated future finances according to return on investment — as we shall cover in subsequent chapters. Don't let calculation of financial ratios distract you from these much more important keys to understanding and analyzing a company's finances.

Still, it is worth your while to understand financial ratios and what they mean. One reason is simply that financial ratios are very widely talked about. A second reason is that ratios provide an especially good method for comparing various aspects of a company's finances with the same aspects of other companies' finances. And a third reason is that financial ratios can provide one insights into various aspects of a particular company's finances.

•

What makes ratios good tools for comparing one company with another is that ratios provide a fair basis for comparing companies of different sizes.

Say that we want to compare Pump & Paddle's first-year net profit with the net profit of another boat company. It is most unlikely that any other boat company we would use for comparison is exactly the same size as Pump & Paddle. It may be that the only other successful inflatable-boat company for which we can get financial reports is Airboat, Inc., a company that is ten years old, has several boat-manufacturing plants across the country, and earns net profit of $500,000 per year.

Obviously, it is not fair to compare little Pump & Paddle's net profit of $21,000 with Airboat's net profit of $500,000; Airboat has so much more with which to make net profit that Pump & Paddle cannot be expected to match Airboat in dollars of net profit.

But if we calculated the return-on-equity ratio for Airboat, and then compared Pump & Paddle to Airboat in terms of this ratio, we would be making a fair comparison — because we would be comparing the two companies in terms of net profit *per dollar of stockholder financing,* and that is fair even if the companies are of very different sizes.

At the start of last year, let's say, Airboat had equity of $4 million. Airboat's return-on-equity ratio would be $500,000 of net profit divided by $4 million of equity, which is 12.5 percent. So Pump & Paddle's higher return on equity of 14 percent indicates that, per dollar of stockholder financing employed to make net profit, little Pump & Paddle earned more net profit than Airboat.

All financial ratios for a company have this fair-comparison feature. That is, the fact that any of a company's ratios is one of the company's financial numbers expressed as a fraction or percentage of another means that the ratio measures a financial number of the company in terms of the company's size. And ratios are easy to calculate. So ratios provide a fair and easy way to compare various aspects of one company's finances with those of other companies.

•

Ratios can also reveal useful things about a company *by itself*.

But to provide useful insights a ratio has to *make sense.* Since it describes the size of one financial item relative to another, a ratio makes sense only if its first financial item is related to its second in a way that makes the relative sizes of the two meaningful.

And to gain the insight that any financial ratio offers, you have to see why the ratio makes sense and what it means.

To illustrate, let's use the financial picture to define a ratio that is useful in helping us assess the amount in one of Pump & Paddle's asset tanks, raw-materials inventory.

From the balance sheet we can see that Pump & Paddle's raw-materials inventory level is $6,000. But this fact alone does not provide enough information for us to determine the adequacy of raw materials. Is $6,000 just right or not enough or too much?

Look at the picture with numbers entered on it:

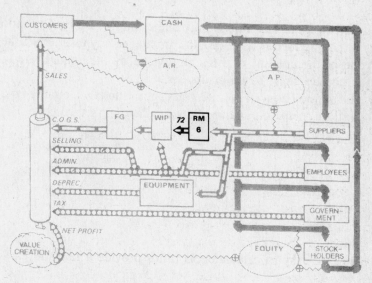

From this picture you can see that the raw-materials inventory is there to supply the outflow from this tank — that is, the flow of rubber from raw materials to work in process, where production of boats begins. And you can also see that, compared to the raw-materials inventory level of $6,000, the rate at which rubber flows from this tank is $72,000 per year.

So a logical ratio that would help us assess the level in this tank is the raw-materials level divided by the annual outflow rate that raw materials supplies. Such a ratio will indicate what fraction of a year's rubber outflow the tank could supply if the company could not buy any more rubber for a while.

This ratio is the $6,000 raw-materials level divided by the $72,000 annual outflow rate, which equals 1/12. The ratio indicates that the raw-materials tank holds enough rubber for 1/12 of a year, or one month. Therefore, if Pump & Paddle suddenly could not purchase any more rubber, the raw-materials inventory tank could keep supplying rubber for production for one more month.

•

This raw-materials ratio is only one example of a type of ratio that can be used in assessing the amount in any asset tank: the ratio of the amount in the tank divided by the annual rate of the outflow that the tank supplies.

From the financial picture you can reason out the same type of ratio to help you analyze Pump & Paddle finished goods:

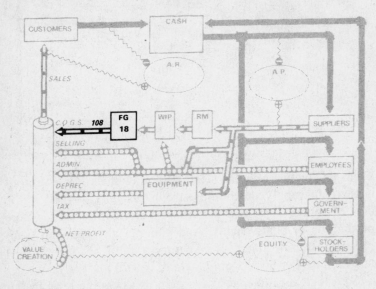

The finished-goods inventory level is there to supply the cost-of-goods-sold outflow (which helps to achieve sales); the level is $18,000, and the outflow it supplies is $108,000 per year. The logical ratio, tank level divided by outflow rate it supplies, is $18,000 divided by $108,000, or 1/6. This ratio indicates that the finished-goods tank contains a supply of 1/6 of a year, or two months; so if for some reason boat production stops, Pump & Paddle will still be able to supply boats for sales for another two months.

From the picture you can develop the same type of ratio for the start-of-year cash level:

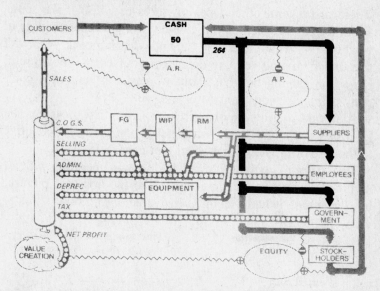

The amount in the cash tank, $50,000, is there to supply the several cash outflows, which are flowing out at a total rate of $264,000 per year. The ratio is the $50,000 cash tank level divided by the $264,000 outflow rate, or about 19 percent. If for some reason cash stops coming in from customers, the amount in the cash tank would be enough for the company to keep making its cash payments for another 19 percent of a year, about 2.3 months.

These ratios do not by themselves give us enough information to determine whether the tank levels are right. To make these evaluations, we have to consider what the amounts of the company's flows may be in the months just ahead, and then use the financial picture to reason out how well the tank levels prepare the company for what may happen just ahead.

However, ratios that compare tank levels to the outflow they supply obviously give us helpful insights, because it *makes sense* to compare a tank level to the outflow it supplies in order to see how long the tank level can supply the outflow.

There are several other types of ratios that also make sense. From a financial picture you can develop an understanding of each type — why it makes sense, and what it means. And with this understanding you can define for yourself the most useful ratios for gaining insights about whatever aspects of a company's finances you want to assess.

A second useful type of ratio is the kind that measures the level of an amount owed — a meter in the picture — relative to the rate of the flows that affect that meter's level.

To illustrate, say that Pump & Paddle was operating with all its flows flowing at the same rates as in the first-year picture, but the company had accounts receivable of $50,000:

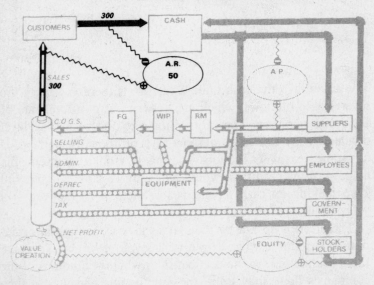

From the picture you can see that this $50,000 meter reading is affected by the flows of sales to customers and payments from customers, and these flows are flowing at the rate of $300,000 per year. So a logical ratio for helping us assess the accounts-receivable level is the $50,000 accounts-receivable level divided by the $300,000 yearly rate of the flows that affect this level, or 1/6.

This ratio indicates that customers owe Pump & Paddle payment for 1/6 of a year or two months of sales. It suggests that on average customers are paying Pump & Paddle for boats two months after buying them. And it also suggests that if for some reason boat sales are suddenly stopped, Pump & Paddle can continue to collect cash from customers at the planned rate for two more months.

The same type of ratio, meter reading divided by rate of flows that affect it, can be used to gain similar insights regarding other amounts owed in or out — such as accounts payable.

•

A third type of useful ratio is that which compares the rate of any of the flows into the sales pump with the rate of the sales outflow that the inflow helps achieve. From this kind of ratio, we can learn which percentages of sales come from the using-up of various things (expenses) and which percentage is net profit.

Look at the flows into and out of the sales pump.

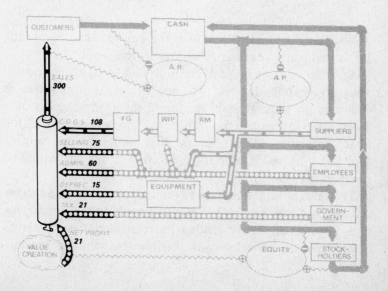

The ratio of net profit to sales is $21,000 divided by $300,000, indicating that net profit is 7 percent of sales. On average, every dollar of sales means 7¢ of net profit, so every $50 boat sale means $3.50 of net profit.

The ratio of cost of goods sold to sales is $108,000 divided by $300,000, or 36 percent. In other words, Pump & Paddle is able to make boats for 36 percent of what it is able to sell them to customers for, leaving the other 64 percent of sales for other expenses and pretax profit. You could compare Pump & Paddle with other companies in this regard. For example, if the same ratio for Airboat is only 25 percent, perhaps Pump & Paddle should devote some attention to exploring the possibility of producing boats for less cost or of raising the selling price.

It is often helpful to turn a ratio upside down. For instance, instead of cost of goods sold divided by sales, calculate sales divided by cost of goods sold: $300,000 divided by $108,000 gives us 2.78. This ratio indicates that customers are willing to pay for the boats 2.78 times what the company is able to make the boats for — another view of the same relationship that the 36 percent represents.

•

A fourth type of helpful ratio is the one that compares tank levels and meter readings in various logical ways.

Say that at start of year Pump & Paddle had the planned asset levels, but also had $25,000 of accounts payable, as shown in the illustration at the top of the next page. It would make sense to compare the amount the company owes with the total amount of value it owns. This would be one way of assessing how well it is positioned to pay off the amount owed if something goes wrong.

The ratio of total liabilities to total assets would be $25,000 divided by $150,000, or 1/6. Or you could turn the ratio upside down: total assets divided by total liabilities equals 6. Either way, the ratio indicates that the company has six dol-

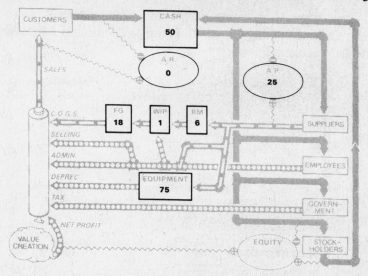

lars of assets owned for every one dollar it owes, suggesting that it is probably in very good position to be able to pay off what it owes even if something serious goes wrong in the months ahead. Airboat may have vastly more assets, totaling $5 million — but if Airboat has liabilities of $4 million, it has only 1.2 dollars of value owned per dollar owed. If so, Airboat may be much less well prepared to promise payoff of all its liabilities.

In this situation the ratio of *current* assets to *current* liabilities — called the *current ratio* — is $75,000 divided by $25,000, or 3. It indicates that for every dollar of liabilities due to be paid off soon, the company has three dollars of assets likely to be converted into cash soon.

•

A fifth type of logical and useful ratio is that which measures a company's sales or profit flow in relation to one of various tank levels or meter readings of value employed to achieve these flows.

For example, compare the Pump & Paddle sales flow with the amount of long-life assets Pump & Paddle has purchased to help achieve the sales:

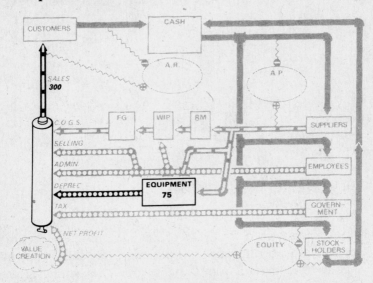

At start of year Pump & Paddle had $75,000 of long-term assets — equipment — and with this amount of long-term assets the company was able to achieve first-year sales of $300,000. The ratio of sales to long-term assets is $300,000 divided by $75,000, which equals 4, indicating that the company is able to achieve four dollars of annual sales per dollar invested in long-term assets.

This ratio, and others of its kind, measure various aspects of a company's effectiveness in using its financing and assets.

Another ratio of this type is the return-on-equity ratio we calculated back at the start of this chapter: first-year net profit of $21,000 divided by start-of-year equity of $150,000 equals 14 percent annual value gain on the stockholder financing employed to achieve the gain.

In financial terms, a company is basically an investment by

its stockholders, who own it. The company is employing stock-holder financing to gain value (make net profit) that can be used either to pay dividends to the stockholders or to expand their company for them. So, among the many ratios, return on equity is the best single ratio for helping you assess a company's overall financial progress over a year.

•

There are many books and courses that provide names, definitions, and formulas for numerous ratios. But the best way to utilize the information to be gleaned from ratios is to understand their logic and meanings, by seeing how each ratio's two parts are related in the financial picture. Through this approach you can define for yourself whatever ratios are most helpful in the assessments you want to make.

Because traditional teaching and practice of financial analysis of companies gives very great emphasis to financial ratios, it is worth re-emphasizing that calculation of ratios is *not* the great secret to understanding and analyzing a company's finances. To understand a company's finances, focus on seeing how all its financial report elements and numbers fit together to provide a financial picture of the company, as described in prior chapters. To assess the company's finances use its picture to think out its financial prospects according to return on investment, as described in the chapters that follow.

· 12 ·

Looking Ahead

WHILE A COMPANY'S financial reports and numbers reflect its past, what concerns investors making decisions today is its future.

But although the reports and numbers a company provides reflect its past, they provide an excellent starting point for assessing its future. Its income statement numbers for last year report the amounts of some of its flows last year, which provide the logical starting point for predicting the amounts of these flows in future years. And its balance sheet numbers for end of last year represent the amounts it owns and owes as it enters the next year.

And, equally important, the financial picture of the company that its reports reflect is just as well suited for working out predictions of a company's financial future as for reporting its past. In other words, you can use a financial picture of a company to work out your own prediction of its future financial numbers as well as to understand its historical numbers.

The numbers we worked out for Pump & Paddle's first year illustrate the point: they could represent predicted numbers prepared before the first year as well as actual numbers reported after the first year.

But to illustrate further, let's say that when the prospective founders provide us the reports for the first year we want to predict the numbers for the company's second year.

We already have the numbers for the balance sheet at start of second year:

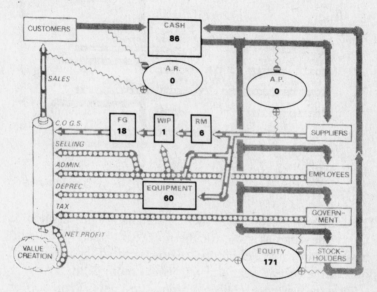

They are exactly the numbers on the balance sheet given us for end of first year.

The numbers for the second-year flows are what we have to predict — they represent what we think the company will do over the second year. Once we have predicted these second-year flows, we can simply calculate the resulting balance sheet levels at end of second year.

Unless we have reason to predict otherwise, our most logical prediction of what the company will do in its second year is that it will repeat what it did in its first year. So for purposes of illustration let's say this is what we predict. Because the flows represent its actions, this would mean that all the company's second-year flows will be the same amounts as the first-year flows, as shown at the top of the next page.

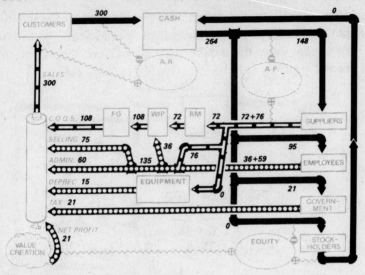

The company's second-year income statement numbers will be exactly the same as those for the first year — sales $300,000 and so on, down to net profit $21,000. And all the unreported flows in the second year will also equal those of the first year — $300,000 of cash collected from customers, $108,000 of completed boats put into finished-goods inventory, and so on.

(If, instead, we had reason to predict that some of the flows will be different in the second year — for example, that sales will increase by 10 percent — we could easily adjust the numbers for second-year flows accordingly. This will be illustrated in the next chapter.)

Now working out the predicted balance sheet numbers for end of second year is simply a matter of calculation: each level at end of year is what it was at start of year, adjusted for whatever changes would be caused by the flows over the year. For example, equipment at end of second year is what it was at start of year, minus depreciation outflow, plus equipment-received inflow.

Since in this particular case the flows that change the levels are the same over the second year as over the first year, the *changes* in the levels from start to end of second year are the same as the changes from start to end of first year:

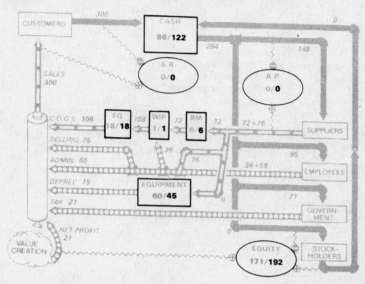

The equipment level drops another $15,000, from $60,000 at start to $45,000 at end, because again in the second year $15,000 flows out as depreciation and no new equipment comes in. The equity level rises another $21,000, from $171,000 at start to $192,000 at end, because again in the second year net profit is $21,000 and no cash flows to or from stockholders. The cash level rises another $36,000, from $86,000 at start to $122,000 at end, because again in the second year $300,000 of cash flows in from customers and $264,000 flows out to suppliers, employees, and government. And all the other levels are left unchanged by the second-year flows, just as they were left unchanged by the same flows in the first year.

Now we can prepare a table of the company's financial report numbers for both first and second years:

INCOME STATEMENT ($000)

	Year 1	Year 2
Sales	$300	$300
Expenses		
Cost of goods sold	108	108
Selling expense	75	75
Administrative expense	60	60
Depreciation	15	15
	$258	$258
Profit before tax	$ 42	$ 42
Tax	21	21
Net profit	$ 21	$ 21

BALANCE SHEET ($000)

	Start of Year 1	End of Year 1	End of Year 2
Assets			
Cash	$ 50	$ 86	$122
Accounts receivable	0	0	0
Inventory			
Finished goods	18	18	18
Work in process	1	1	1
Raw materials	6	6	6
	$ 25	$ 25	$ 25
Equipment	75	60	45
Total	$150	$171	$192
Liabilities & Equity			
Accounts payable	$ 0	$ 0	$ 0
Equity	150	171	192
Total	$150	$171	$192

In this table, the income statement numbers represent flows over the two years, and the balance sheet numbers represent levels at starts and ends of the years. The numbers for the first-year income statement and the balance sheets at start and end of first year are those provided to us by the prospective founders of Pump & Paddle; those for the second-year income statement and end-of-second-year balance sheet are the ones we worked out on the financial picture based on our predictions.

•

We can use the financial picture to predict a company's financial report numbers for any number of years — two or five or ten or twenty.

For example, since the longest-term step Pump & Paddle takes at its start is to purchase equipment expected to last through year five, we may decide to extend our predictions through the company's fifth year. If we predict that in each of the five years the company will repeat exactly what it does in its first year, our predictions of its report numbers through year five would look like this:

INCOME STATEMENT ($000)

	Year 1	Year 2	Year 3	Year 4	Year 5
Sales	$300	$300	$300	$300	$300
Expenses					
Cost of goods sold	108	108	108	108	108
Selling expense	75	75	75	75	75
Administrative expense	60	60	60	60	60
Depreciation	15	15	15	15	15
	$258	$258	$258	$258	$258
Profit before tax	$ 42	$ 42	$ 42	$ 42	$ 42
Tax	21	21	21	21	21
Net profit	$ 21	$ 21	$ 21	$ 21	$ 21

(reports continued at top of next page)

BALANCE SHEET ($000)

	Start of Year 1	End of Year 1	End of Year 2	End of Year 3	End of Year 4	End of Year 5
Assets						
Cash	$ 50	$ 86	$122	$158	$194	$230
Accounts receivable	0	0	0	0	0	0
Inventory						
Finished goods	18	18	18	18	18	18
Work in process	1	1	1	1	1	1
Raw materials	6	6	6	6	6	6
	$ 25	$ 25	$ 25	$ 25	$ 25	$ 25
Equipment	75	60	45	30	15	0
Total	$150	$171	$192	$213	$234	$255
Liabilities & equity						
Accounts payable	$ 0	$ 0	$ 0	$ 0	$ 0	$ 0
Equity	150	171	192	213	234	255
Total	$150	$171	$192	$213	$234	$255

Each year's income-statement numbers are exactly the same as those of the first year, because these numbers represent flows we predict will be repeated each year. As a result of each year's flows, the balance sheet numbers keep changing from start to end of each year; but because each year's flows are the same, the levels change by the same amount each year.

Each year the equipment level drops by $15,000, because each year $15,000 of depreciation flows out but no new equipment value flows in. Each year the equity level rises by $21,000, because the net profit flow is $21,000 and no cash flows from or to stockholders. Each year the cash level rises by $36,000, because each year $300,000 of cash is received from customers and $264,000 of cash is paid out to suppliers, employees, and government. And each year all of the other levels remain unchanged, just as they did in the first year.

As a result, over the five years the equipment level drops by $75,000 (five times $15,000), from $75,000 at start of first year to zero by end of fifth year. The equity level rises by $105,000 (five times $21,000), from $150,000 at start of first year to $255,000 by end of fifth year. The cash level rises by $180,000 (five times $36,000), from $50,000 at start of first year to $230,000 by end of fifth year. And all the other balance sheet levels are still the same at end of fifth year as they were at start of first year.

While this five-year sequence of reports is predicted, it could as well be actual reports — it shows what the company's actual reports will be if our predictions come true. Whether you are looking back at a company's history or forward at its predicted future, you can see the company's development more clearly in a sequence of reports for several years than in reports for a single year.

Almost every company takes some action that requires years to complete, so a sequence of reports covering the entire action from start to finish will show the process clearly. For example, Pump & Paddle's equipment purchase starts a five-year process for using the equipment to deliver sales and collect cash for the sales. In any single year's reports you can see only a short part of this process — only one fifth of the equipment used up to achieve one year's sales and resulting cash gain. But from the full sequence of reports, from start-up through year five, you can see the entire process, which begins with the company owning new equipment plus $50,000 of cash and ends with the equipment fully used up and the company holding $255,000 of cash.

A second and more valuable advantage of looking at reports for a sequence of years rather than for a single year is that you can see trends in the amounts of a company's flows. Our table shows each flow the same amount year after year, but it is much more common for a company's flows to increase each year. For example, Pump & Paddle sales might rise by 15 percent per year as the company learns to make and sell boats more efficiently, and cost per production worker might rise by 8 percent per year. If we were predicting the company's future after Pump & Paddle completed its first three years, and we looked at only the reports for the just-completed third year, we would not be able to see anything about the trends in the amounts of the company's flows. But by looking at the sequence of reports for all three years we would be able to see whether the flows have been the same each year. If they were not the same, we could tell how much each flow has increased or decreased from year to year, and this would obviously be valuable information for us to consider in predicting the amounts of the company's flows in future years.

But, as we observed earlier, the most fundamental thing that the table illustrates is that the financial report system can be used to predict a company's financial future, as a basis for judging the potential future the company may offer an investor considering buying some of its shares or giving it a loan.

The table shows that if the company keeps repeating its planned first-year actions each year, at the end of the five years the company would have $230,000 of cash. If it intended to stay in business it would have to replace its original equipment, perhaps again paying $75,000, and it would want to continue holding $50,000 in its cash tank as advised by the accountant. But this would leave the other $105,000 of its cash free for the company to use for paying dividends to the stockholders who provided the initial $150,000, or for investment in improvements of the company that would be expected to lead to considerably more profit, cash, and dividends farther in the future.

If, back when we were first presented the proposal to invest in Pump & Paddle start-up and the accountant's predicted reports for the company's first year, we translated our predictions for the company into future financial report numbers, we would have in front of us the best numbers we can develop

on the company for assessing investment in it. In the same
way, for any established company with actual historical reports
you can translate your predictions of its future actions into
predictions of its future financial results.

· 13 ·

What If ... ?

IN THE SAME WAY that you can figure out what a company's future financial reports will be if it meets your predictions, you can also figure out how these future reports would be changed if the company *deviates* from your predictions in various ways.

For example, we might expect that Pump & Paddle will probably perform approximately as predicted in the previous chapter, but we might think there is some possibility that over the first year the company will improve its boat-making quality enough to raise its selling price by $5 at the start of the second year and still keep selling 6,000 boats each year. If so, we could develop a second prediction for the five years' reports that would look like this:

INCOME STATEMENT ($000)

	Year 1	Year 2	Year 3	Year 4	Year 5
Sales	$300	$330	$330	$330	$330
Expenses					
Cost of goods sold	108	108	108	108	108
Selling expense	75	75	75	75	75
Administrative expense	60	60	60	60	60
Depreciation	15	15	15	15	15
	$258	$258	$258	$258	$258
Profit before tax	$ 42	$ 72	$ 72	$ 72	$ 72
Tax	21	36	36	36	36
Net profit	$ 21	$ 36	$ 36	$ 36	$ 36

BALANCE SHEET ($000)

	Start of Year 1	End of Year 1	End of Year 2	End of Year 3	End of Year 4	End of Year 5
Assets						
Cash	$ 50	$ 86	$137	$188	$239	$290
Accounts receivable	0	0	0	0	0	0
Inventory						
Finished goods	18	18	18	18	18	18
Work in process	1	1	1	1	1	1
Raw materials	6	6	6	6	6	6
	$ 25	$ 25	$ 25	$ 25	$ 25	$ 25
Equipment	75	60	45	30	15	0
Total	$150	$171	$207	$243	$279	$315
Liabilities & equity						
Accounts payable	$ 0	$ 0	$ 0	$ 0	$ 0	$ 0
Equity	150	171	207	243	279	315
Total	$150	$171	$207	$243	$279	$315

On the income statement, in year two and each subsequent year sales are $330,000 instead of $300,000, because with 6,000 boats sold each year the $5 selling-price increase adds $30,000 to sales. And, since expenses are unchanged, in each of these years tax and net profit are each $15,000 higher than in the first year, each $36,000 instead of $21,000.

On the balance sheet, in each of years two through five the equity level rises $36,000 instead of $21,000, because net profit is $36,000 per year. And in each of these years the cash level rises an extra $15,000, up $51,000 each year instead of $36,000, because in each of these years the company receives an extra $30,000 from customers and pays an extra $15,000 for tax on the increased profit — receiving $330,000 from customers and paying a total of $279,000 to suppliers, employees, and government.

These reports show that if the company carries out our prediction with the price increase, it will have an additional $60,000 of cash at the end — $290,000 instead of $230,000. So if it then spends $75,000 to replace its equipment and keeps

$50,000 in cash to continue operating, it would have an extra $165,000 that it could use for dividends or for improvements expected to lead to more profit and dividends later.

•

Another possibility we might want to look at is that Pump & Paddle is not able to sell the full 6,000 boats each year, especially if it increases the price. If, after the price increase is made at start of year two, the company sells only 5,000 boats each year, and the company adjusts its production, purchases, and labor so that only 5,000 boats are made each year and the inventories are kept at the planned levels, its reports for the five years will look like this, as shown at the top of next page. On the income statement for each of years two through five, sales are 5,000 boats times the $55 price, which is $275,000, and cost of goods sold is 5,000 boats times $18, which is $90,000. With other expenses unchanged, profit before tax is $35,000, so tax and net profit is each $17,500.

As a result, on the balance sheet in each of these years equity rises by $17,500, because there is net profit of that amount. And in each of these years the cash level rises by $32,500. This cash rise is $3,500 below that in the original prediction: the inflow of cash from customers is $25,000 less, and the total outflow of cash is $21,500 less — $18,000 less to suppliers and employees for rubber and production labor, and $3,500 less to government for tax. The total annual cash flows are $275,000 in from customers, and a total of $242,500 out — to suppliers and employees $90,000 to replace boats and $135,000 for selling and administration, to government $17,500 for tax.

This table shows that even if the price increase reduces boat sales from 6,000 to 5,000 per year, by the end of the fifth year the company will still have $216,000 of cash. So if it then spends $75,000 to replace equipment and reserves $50,000 of cash for subsequent operations, it would still have $91,000 of extra cash for dividends or improvements — nearly as much

INCOME STATEMENT ($000)

	Year 1	Year 2	Year 3	Year 4	Year 5
Sales	$300	$275	$275	$275	$275
Expenses					
Cost of goods sold	108	90	90	90	90
Selling expense	75	75	75	75	75
Administrative expense	60	60	60	60	60
Depreciation	15	15	15	15	15
	$258	$240	$240	$240	$240
Profit before tax	$ 42	$ 35	$ 35	$ 35	$ 35
Tax	21	17.5	17.5	17.5	17.5
Net profit	$ 21	$ 17.5	$ 17.5	$ 17.5	$ 17.5

BALANCE SHEET ($000)

	Start of Year 1	End of Year 1	End of Year 2	End of Year 3	End of Year 4	End of Year 5
Assets						
Cash	$ 50	$ 86	$118.5	$151.0	$183.5	$216.0
Accounts receivable	0	0	0.0	0.0	0.0	0.0
Inventory						
Finished goods	18	18	18.0	18.0	18.0	18.0
Work in process	1	1	1.0	1.0	1.0	1.0
Raw materials	6	6	6.0	6.0	6.0	6.0
	$ 25	$ 25	$ 25.0	$ 25.0	$ 25.0	$ 25.0
Equipment	75	60	45.0	30.0	15.0	0.0
Total	$150	$171	$188.5	$206.0	$223.5	$241.0
Liabilities & equity						
Accounts payable	$ 0	$ 0	$ 0.0	$ 0.0	$ 0.0	$ 0.0
Equity	150	171	188.5	206.0	223.5	241.0
Total	$150	$171	$188.5	$206.0	$223.5	$241.0

as the $106,000 available for these purposes if there is no price increase and sales stay at 6,000 boats per year.

It could very well be that we predict a range of possibilities for Pump & Paddle: the company will probably perform as predicted earlier, but might raise its price $5 in which case annual boat sales could be any number from 5,000 to 6,000.

If so, our three tables would show how much the company could have available for dividends over the first five years: probably about $105,000, but perhaps as little as $91,000 or as much as $165,000.

·

We could apply the relationships shown in the financial picture to prepare future reports reflecting any combination of events we might hypothesize for Pump & Paddle's future — the plan modified by an increase in labor cost, or the plan modified by both a price increase and a strike in the rubber industry, for example.

This is the *most* valuable use of the financial report system for all decision-makers — for the people managing a company, as well as for the people considering investing in a company. A decision-maker can never be sure just what may happen to a company. By making several sets of predictions and then working out the future financial report results for each, he or she can see what the financial results would be for each possibility, and can gain a good sense of the range of possibilities for the company's financial future.

· 14 ·

Evaluating Company Finances

ONCE YOU HAVE developed financial projections for a business, you still need a good measure for evaluating the projected results — to decide for or against investing if you are an investor, or to select the best plan for the business if you are a manager.

The best measure for financial evaluation of investments and businesses is the *present value* method of measuring return on investment. In this chapter we will describe and illustrate its calculation, meaning, and use, and for the illustrations we will look at Pump & Paddle from the viewpoint of outsiders considering investment in the company's stock. But if you are involved in management of a business, or plan to become a manager, keep in mind that the same method is equally well suited for evaluation of a company's own investments, projects, and overall plans.

To illustrate the present value method, say that you now have $15,000 to invest and are deciding whether to invest this money in the start-up of Pump & Paddle or in a bank where it would earn 10 percent interest.

To raise the $150,000 it needs, Pump & Paddle will sell 1,000 shares at $150 each, so with your $15,000 you could buy 100 shares of Pump & Paddle. You predict that Pump & Paddle will follow our first five-year prediction — that it will

PRESENT VALUE DISCOUNT FACTORS

Annual Rate of Return

Year	6%	8%	10%	12%	14%	16%	18%	20%	25%	30%	35%	40%	45%	50%
1	.943	.926	.909	.893	.877	.862	.847	.833	.800	.769	.741	.714	.690	.667
2	.890	.857	.826	.797	.769	.743	.718	.694	.640	.592	.549	.510	.476	.444
3	.840	.794	.751	.712	.675	.641	.609	.579	.512	.455	.406	.364	.328	.296
4	.792	.735	.683	.636	.592	.552	.516	.482	.410	.350	.301	.260	.226	.198
5	.747	.681	.621	.567	.519	.476	.437	.402	.328	.269	.223	.186	.156	.132
6	.705	.630	.564	.507	.456	.410	.370	.335	.262	.207	.165	.133	.108	.088
7	.665	.583	.513	.452	.400	.354	.314	.279	.210	.159	.122	.095	.074	.059
8	.627	.540	.467	.404	.351	.305	.266	.233	.168	.123	.091	.068	.051	.039
9	.592	.500	.424	.361	.308	.263	.225	.194	.134	.094	.067	.048	.035	.026
10	.558	.463	.386	.322	.270	.227	.191	.162	.107	.073	.050	.035	.024	.017
15	.417	.315	.239	.183	.140	.108	.084	.065	.035	.020	.011	.006	.004	.002
20	.312	.215	.149	.104	.073	.051	.037	.026	.012	.005	.002	.001	.001	.000
25	.233	.146	.092	.059	.038	.024	.016	.010	.004	.001	.001	.000	.000	.000

do the same each year for five years and end the fifth year with $230,000 of cash and $25,000 of inventory. And you predict that after these five years, when the equipment is used up, Pump & Paddle will simply close down, by selling its inventories to another boat company for the $25,000 they cost and then giving all of its $255,000 back to its stockholders.

Since you would own 100 of Pump & Paddle's 1,000 shares, at the end of the fifth year you would get back $25,500. The question, then, is whether investing $15,000 now and getting back $25,500 five years later beats the 10 percent interest that the $15,000 would earn at the bank.

There are several ways to make this calculation, but by using the present value method you can do it with only one multiplication. This multiplication will show you how much you'd have to invest in the bank at 10 percent now in order to get back what an investment of $15,000 in Pump & Paddle would provide you — $25,500 five years later. If to get the same return from the bank you'd have to invest more than $15,000, the predicted Pump & Paddle investment is better than the bank's 10 percent. But if you could get the same return by putting less than $15,000 in the bank, the Pump & Paddle investment is not as good as the bank's 10 percent.

To make this calculation, you would use a number from the table of "present value discount factors" on the page at left.

The vertical columns labeled across the top of the table represent various rates of return that you may be able to get from other investments, such as the bank's 10 percent, and the horizontal rows labeled down the left represent years in the future. You can see, for example, that the discount factor number for five years in the future at a 10 percent return rate is 0.621.

What this number means is that, investing at 10 percent, the amount you invest now is 0.621 of the amount you could get back five years later. For example, to get back $1,000 five years from now you have to invest $621 at 10 percent.

So, to calculate how much you have to invest at 10 percent now to get $25,500 five years from now, simply multiply $25,500 by the discount factor for year five in the 10 percent column. That is, the amount you would have to invest is $25,500 times 0.621, which equals $15,835.

This amount, $15,835, is called the present value of $25,500 received five years from now for somebody who can invest at 10 percent. It means that if you could invest at 10 percent and somebody owed you $25,500 payable five years from now, you'd just as soon have $15,835 now instead, because if you invested that amount at 10 percent now it would grow to $25,500 by the end of five years.

Since this number of $15,835 represents the amount you would have to invest in the bank at 10 percent now to get back $25,500 five years later, and according to prediction the investment in Pump & Paddle will provide you the same return for a smaller investment of only $15,000, the predicted return of the Pump & Paddle investment is better than the 10 percent offered by the bank.

.

Present value is a superb method for evaluating the predicted results of any investment. Simply use discount factors from the column of the table representing the rate of return you can get elsewhere, and calculate the present value of the predicted future returns from the investment you are considering. If the present value of an investment's predicted future returns is more than the amount to be invested now, that investment's predicted returns are better than the rate at which you can invest elsewhere. If the present value of the returns is less than the investment, the investment's returns are not as good as the rate at which you can invest elsewhere.

The beauty of this method of analysis is that it is a mathematically perfect way to compare an investment's results with the rate at which you can invest elsewhere, yet it involves only a few simple calculations, even if the investment you are considering will deliver a complicated sequence of future returns.

For example, let's predict that Pump & Paddle will do just as described above, except that instead of paying you the entire $25,500 at the end of year five it will pay you one fifth of this amount at the end of each of the five years — $5,100 each year.

Here is the calculation of the present value of all the five years' returns:

Year	Cash flow	10% Discount factor		Present value of cash flow
1	$5,100	× 0.909	=	$ 4,636
2	5,100	× 0.826	=	4,213
3	5,100	× 0.751	=	3,830
4	5,100	× 0.683	=	3,483
5	5,100	× 0.621	=	3,167
		Net present value	=	$19,329

The present value of each year's return is the $5,100 you receive that year multiplied by the discount factor for that year from the 10 percent column of the discount factor table. To calculate the total present value of the returns of all five years, just add up the present values of the five individual years' returns.

The calculation shows that the present value of the returns from the Pump & Paddle investment would be $19,329. This means that to get the same returns at the same times by investing now in the bank at 10 percent, you would have to invest $19,329. Since in the Pump & Paddle investment you can get these returns with a smaller investment, only $15,000, the Pump & Paddle investment is a bargain compared with an investment in the bank at 10 percent.

In this second Pump & Paddle investment example, the

present value of the future returns is higher than that for the
first example — $19,329 compared with $15,835 — even
though the total amount of cash you get back from Pump &
Paddle is $25,500 in each example. But it should be higher,
because the second example's returns are better for you. It is
important to you not only how much cash you get back from
Pump & Paddle but also how soon you get it back, because the
sooner you get back some of the $25,500, the sooner you can
put it in the bank at 10 percent to earn more return. The very
purpose of the present value method is to evaluate future returns in terms of both how much and how soon. And the reason
that the second example's returns have a higher present value
than the first example's returns is that in the second example
you receive most of the return sooner.

Consider a third example. Say you predict that Pump &
Paddle will need some time to get up to speed in its boat operations, and as a result the dividends you get from it will be
zero the first year, $1,000 the second year, $4,000 the third
year, and $5,100 in each of years four and five. Without the
present value discount factors, you would have to do a lot of
calculating to determine whether all these dividend figures add
up to better than a 10 percent return on your $15,000 invest-
ment. But with the discount factors it is easy to calculate:

Year	Cash flow		10% Discount factor		Present value of cash flow
1	$ 0	×	0.909	=	$ 0
2	1,000	×	0.826	=	826
3	4,000	×	0.751	=	3,004
4	5,100	×	0.683	=	3,483
5	5,100	×	0.621	=	3,167
			Net present value	=	$10,480

The present value of all these future returns is less than the
$15,000 you would have to invest in Pump & Paddle now to
get them; it is only $10,480. That means you could get the

same returns at the same times by investing now only $10,480 at 10 percent in the bank. So if these returns are what investment of $15,000 in Pump & Paddle will deliver, it would be better to put the money in the bank at 10 percent.

By providing you a number for the present value of the future return you predict for a company's shares, the present value method shows you what the shares are worth right now according to your predictions. So by comparing the present value of the predicted future returns with the price at which you can now buy or sell the shares, you can see whether your prediction indicates the share's present price is a bargain or an excessive price.

For example, say you are analyzing a big company whose shares are traded on the stock market, and the future dividends you predict for one share represent a present value of $100. This would mean that if your predictions are about right the share is now worth about $100. If its price on the stock market is now only $80, you should keep the shares you have and buy more, but if its present price is $120 you should sell any shares you own and not buy any shares now.

•

Most companies use a fraction of the gain from each year's net profit to pay cash dividends that year, keeping the rest for company investment. On the surface, it would appear that the higher the fraction of net profit used to pay dividends, the better for the stockholders. But in a case where a company can invest very profitably, it is better for the stockholders if the company uses a *lower* fraction of each year's net profit for dividends!

Through present value calculations, you can see very clearly the advantage to stockholders of a very profitable company's keeping its dividend fraction of net profit low.

To illustrate, let's say again that the Pump & Paddle stockholders can invest at 10 percent, and let's define a situation in which Pump & Paddle could invest to make its profit grow. Say that after some initial growth Pump & Paddle's net profit has leveled off at $100,000 per year and if the company doesn't invest any more its net profit will continue to be $100,000 per year forever. And say that Pump & Paddle is now capable of investing any amounts at any time at 16 percent, so that if, for example, it invests $10,000 next year, this investment will produce $1,600 of extra net profit every year thereafter.

Now, say that at the annual stockholders' meeting Pump & Paddle management has outlined two plans for dividend payments and has asked the stockholders to choose between the plans. Plan A calls for the company to use all of each year's net profit for dividends. Plan B calls for the company to use only half of each year's net profit for dividends and to invest the other half at 16 percent to increase future profit. Which plan should the stockholders vote for?

If the stockholders choose Plan A, with all of each year's net profit used for dividends, net profit will continue to be $100,000 each year, because nothing will be invested by the company to increase it. And dividends will be $100,000 every year, because each year's dividends are all of that year's net profit.

But if the stockholders vote for Plan B, net profit will grow by 8 percent per year. The first year, net profit will be $100,000, as it would have been in Plan A. But that year the company will invest $50,000 of this net profit at 16 percent, and this will add $8,000 to the second year's net profit, raising it 8 percent, from $100,000 to $108,000. And so on.

In Plan B, dividends will be only $50,000 next year. But since each year they are half of net profit, and net profit will increase by 8 percent per year, dividends will also increase by 8 percent per year. Dividends will be $50,000 next year, $54,000 the following year, and so on.

Here is a graph comparing both net profit and dividends for the two plans over the next twenty years:

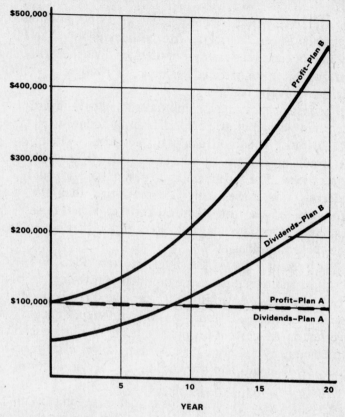

YEAR

In Plan A, dividends are $100,000 per year forever; in Plan B, they start at only $50,000 but grow by 8 percent per year and become greater than $100,000 within about nine years.

In this case, the dividends from Plan B represent a higher present value to the stockholders than those of Plan A. If we use 10 percent discount factors, representing the rate at which the stockholders can invest elsewhere, we can calculate the present value of Plan A's dividends of $100,000 per year forever to be exactly $1 million. The present value of receiving all the growing future dividends of Plan B is much higher — $2.5 million.

So Plan B, with only half of each year's net profit used for dividends, is certainly better for the stockholders than Plan A with all of each year's net profit used for dividends!

However, if Pump & Paddle could not invest very profitably, Plan A would be better.

For instance, say that Pump & Paddle could invest at only 8 percent instead of 16 percent. Then by following Plan B — that is, investing half of each year's net profit — Pump & Paddle would make its net profit and dividends grow by only 4 percent instead of 8 percent. Even at this slow growth rate the dividends would eventually become larger than the steady $100,000 per year from Plan A, but the dividends from Plan B would not grow fast enough to represent a higher present value than those from Plan A.

The present value of the dividends from Plan B, $50,000 next year and then 4 percent more each year thereafter, is only about $830,000, obviously less than the $1 million present value of the dividends from Plan A. So if Pump & Paddle could invest at only 8 percent it would be better for the stockholders if the company followed Plan A, using all of each year's net profit for dividends and not keeping any net profit for investment.

What this example illustrates is that at a company that is capable of investing very profitably it is better for the stockholders if the percentage of net profit that the company uses for dividends is low rather than high. In a nutshell, the reason this is true is that, by not paying a dollar of dividends now, the company can use the dollar profitably enough to deliver much higher future dividends that represent a present value of more than a dollar.

In general, companies operate according to this principle, and in general investors evaluate company stocks according to this principle. The companies that can invest most profitably usually do use relatively small percentages of their net profit for dividends, keeping most of it for investment to achieve much higher future profit and dividends. And for exactly the same reason investors generally show their approval of this situation by bidding for shares of stock. If two companies are now earning about the same net profit, and one uses most for dividends but the other invests very profitably and uses only a small percentage for dividends, investors will by and large be willing to bid more for the second company's stock, because they expect the second company's low but rapidly growing dividends to be worth more than the first company's high but nongrowing dividends.

•

If you plan to hold some shares for just a few years and can predict when you will sell them and just about how much you will receive from selling them, you should include the present value of the amount you expect to receive from selling them along with the present value of the dividends you expect to receive while owning them.*

Otherwise the best way to calculate the present value of a share is to predict all its dividends forever and calculate their present value. Fortunately, in most cases you can determine approximately what this number is by predicting dividends and calculating their present values for only a limited number of years, because the farther in the future are dividend dollars the smaller are their present values.

But if you can reduce your prediction of a share's future

* You will probably have to pay different tax rates on various types of cash return from investments. For example, in this case, only part of what you receive from sale of the shares would be taxed, probably at a relatively low long-term capital gains rate, but your dividend receipts would probably all be taxed at a higher "ordinary income" rate. Since tax affects what you really gain, it is best to use after-tax numbers for all returns in your present value calculations, including the rate at which you can invest elsewhere as well as the dollar returns from the investment you are evaluating. In this chapter we have neglected the investor's tax because each reader will have a different tax situation, and our purpose is to provide simple and clear examples of the present value method rather than to explain how to calculate your taxes.

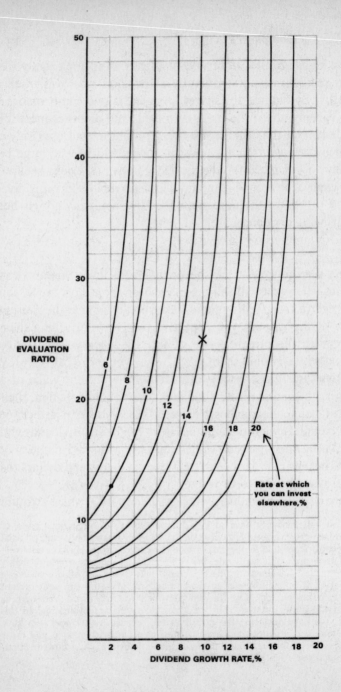

DIVIDEND
EVALUATION
RATIO

Rate at which
you can invest
elsewhere,%

DIVIDEND GROWTH RATE,%

dividends to a predicted annual rate of growth — such as a growth rate of 6 percent per year forever, or the same every year forever (0 percent growth rate) — you can calculate the present value of all the predicted dividends forever simply by multiplying the present annual dividend by a number that we will call a *dividend evaluation ratio*.

The mathematical reasoning to figure out this ratio for various situations would be somewhat challenging for most people, so rather than explain the mathematics we have prepared a graph from which you can merely read off the ratio for various situations, shown on the page at the left.

The curved lines on the graph represent various rates at which you may be able to invest elsewhere, and the horizontal axis has a scale of annual rates at which you might predict a share's dividends will grow. To find the point on the graph for evaluating a particular share, move along the line representing the rate at which you can invest elsewhere until you are directly above the mark representing the annual rate at which you expect the share's dividends to grow.

Then move straight across to the left axis to find the dividend evaluation ratio for that share. This ratio multiplied by the share's present annual dividend equals the present value of all the future dividends that you predict for that share forever.

For example, say you can invest elsewhere at 10 percent, and you predict a share's dividend will grow by 2 percent per year forever, and the share's present annual dividend is $10. On the graph you can see that the curve representing your other investments' 10 percent rate of return passes directly above the 2 percent growth rate that you predict for this dividend at the point marked by a small dot on the graph, which is at a height that indicates a dividend evaluation ratio of about 12.5 on the axis at the left. So the present value of all the share's predicted future dividends is this ratio of 12.5 times the present annual dividend of $10, which equals $125. If your predictions are right, the share is worth $125.

Or say that you can invest elsewhere at 14 percent, and for a share with a present annual dividend of $20 you predict an annual dividend growth rate of 10 percent forever. On the graph, the curve representing the 14 percent at which you can invest elsewhere passes above the 10 percent on the horizontal axis representing the growth rate you predict for the dividends at the point marked by a small x, and this point is at a height that indicates a dividend evaluation ratio of about 25 on the left axis. Then the present value of all the future dividends you predict for this share forever is this ratio of 25 times the present annual dividend of $20, which equals $500. If your predictions are on target, the share is worth $500.

For any share whose dividends you expect will grow at a steady rate forever, or will stay the same forever (which amounts to a 0 percent growth rate), you can use this graph to calculate the present value of all the predicted dividends forever according to the shortcut method illustrated by the two preceding examples.

•

Whatever you predict for a company, once you have predicted its financial future you can use the present value method to calculate what its predicted future is worth now. To evaluate one share of the company, just calculate the present value of all the cash you predict you will receive in the future from your ownership of the share. The present value calculation can be done quickly and easily, and it provides you a mathematically perfect measure of today's worth of the company's predicted future.

Predicting a company's financial future is of course much more challenging. But, as we have seen, the financial report system provides a marvelously valuable and usable basis for predicting the future finances of a company. By seeing a company's historical reports as reflections of a financial picture of the company, in which all the parts fit together very logically, you can see what the report numbers say about the company's past actions and its resulting status. You can use the report numbers to figure out for yourself the financial actions of the company that were not reported, including its flows of cash. With this understanding of what the company did over past years and how it stood at the end of last year, you will have a basis for predicting what it is likely to do in future years. And you can use the financial picture that the reports reflect to figure out the future financial reports that will result according to any predictions you may have made about what the company might do or have done to it. This will enable you to turn your entire analysis into the best possible prediction of how much cash you may get back, and when, if you invest.

Although the future always promises surprises, and virtually every prediction of a company is bound to be off by at least a little, you can use financial reports to improve your predictions for investments just as investment specialists and company managers do. And for you, as for them, the best investment of all is a few hours spent with the financial reports and numbers before you invest a lot of your money in the companies that the reports and numbers describe so well.

· 15 ·

Who Profits from Profit?

IN THIS final chapter, let's step back and consider what profit means to society at large. We have been discussing both the company itself and its stockholders, and it is obvious that they both want the company to make high profit. But a company affects many other parties: organizations, such as suppliers, lenders, and government; and, more important, people, such as customers and employees. What does its profit mean to them?

On the financial reports, profit appears to be value "left over" for a company — something that is not really necessary for the company's serving of its customers and employees. People very often talk of high profit as if it were something taken from customers or employees and given to the company's owners.

But in fact a company's making profit *is* necessary for it to serve its customers and employees, and is in the interests of its customers and employees as much as its owners — and the higher the profit the better for them all. By looking at profit in the context of the whole financial picture of a company, and thinking about how the company's profit is related to its serving customers and employees in competition with other companies, you can see how profit arms and motivates a company to serve customers and employees.

·

Basically, a company is a long-term investment of its stock-holders. And its net profit for a year is basically the return on the stockholders' investment that the company earned over that year. So the best way to measure whether the profit is high or low is to determine whether it represents high or low return on the stockholder investment employed to make the profit.

Exactly what a company's equity represents is the amount of stockholder investment that the company holds. It includes the amount that the stockholders have given the company, and also all net profit the company has made for the stockholders in the past and kept to employ in making more profit. Therefore, the best way to measure a company's profit for a year is the return-on-equity ratio discussed in Chapter 11. Calculate this ratio to measure the percentage return on stockholder investment that the profit represents. Then compare this percentage with those of other companies to see whether the profit represents high or low company return on the stockholder investment in it.

As we have seen, return on equity for Pump & Paddle's first year is $21,000 net profit for the year divided by $150,000 equity at start of year, which comes to a 14 percent return on stockholder investment.

On the average, all United States manufacturing companies achieve annual return on equity of about 16 percent. Pump & Paddle has certainly done well to come close to the return on equity of established companies in its very first year, but compared with other companies its net profit is neither very low nor very high.

•

Notice where profit comes from and where it goes on the financial picture.

Net profit is not just something left over — it is truly value that a company creates, and adds to the world's economy, by making the products and services it delivers to customers worth more than the things it uses up to deliver them. If by using up $279,000 in expenses and tax Pump & Paddle can deliver boats that customers are willing to pay $300,000 for, Pump & Paddle is indeed creating the other $21,000 of value put into the boats.

(If a particular company holds a monopolistic position, and is thus able to charge excessively high prices because it has no competition, or if a company causes more social damage than its taxes cover, such as heavy pollution, that company's net profit is not all really value it has created. But most companies have to offer competitive prices to make sales. And most companies provide major social benefits — such as employment, as well as the payment of taxes — that more than compensate for any adverse social effects of their operations. So for most companies most of the time net profit is a very good measure of the value the company has really created and added to the economy and society.)

The picture also shows that profit is *not* cash paid to the owners.

Net profit is a component of the value that a company puts into the sales flowing to customers; it is not value flowing to owners. And the party that receives the cash payment for a company's profit is the company, not the owners.

After making net profit, a company may use some of the resulting cash gain to pay cash dividends to its owners — but, as the picture shows, dividends are not at all the same as net profit, and a company's dividends are usually much smaller than its profit. In general, companies use more of their cash gain from profit for investments that improve and expand their products for customers and jobs for employees than they use to pay dividends to their owners.

What a company pays to its owners is dividends, not net profit. So if any part of a company's finances can be called value taken from customers and employees and given to owners, it is the company's dividends, not its profit.

.

Because of competition, a company cannot keep serving customers and employees without profit — it *has* to make profit, high profit, to keep serving customers and employees effectively.

To illustrate, consider the kind of competition we would face if we started Pump & Paddle.

When we start the company, we will create a new competitive threat to other boat companies, and will win some customers and some employees from other companies. Say that, once we have started, the company does just well enough each year so that it has neither profit nor loss — each year sales just equal expenses, so there is no tax and no net profit. In a typical individual year the company's cash level will still rise by $15,000, because that year's sales delivered and collected for will include $15,000 from equipment depreciation that was paid for earlier. But every fifth year, when the equipment unit wears out, the company will have to spend $75,000 for a new unit. So over the long term the company will receive just enough cash to stay in exactly the same position.

But sooner or later other boat companies will take new competitive steps that threaten to win back customers and employees from Pump & Paddle. Another boat company that is making profit may use the resulting extra cash to develop a new attachment to its boat-making equipment, a device that permits this company to produce twice as many boats with only one more employee. With this improvement, the second company could afford to offer boats like those of Pump & Paddle at a lower price, or to add a new feature to its boats and offer better boats at the same price as those of Pump & Paddle. This company could also afford to offer each employee more pay, because with the equipment attachment its employees would be able to produce more or better boats per employee.

And a third boat company that is also making profit might use its extra cash to develop and introduce a new style of boat that can be produced for the same cost but is more appealing to customers than Pump & Paddle's boat design, so that even when sold at a higher price the third company's boats are more attractive to customers. With its boats selling at a higher price, this third company could also afford to offer higher pay to attract employees.

Without profit, Pump & Paddle will collect only enough cash from customers to maintain the same financial status. Without profit, Pump & Paddle will not be collecting any more cash from customers than it has to pay to other outsiders to just stay the same. And because of the company's lack of profit, potential investors will probably be unwilling to give the company the cash it needs for the improvements. They will see that the company is not making profit from the money the original investors provided, and thus is unable to pay the original investors dividends on their investment or make improvements that could lead to future dividends for them. The potential new investors will probably conclude that the company would not use any additional investment well enough to pay return to them, and they will probably decide to leave their money in the bank, where it is earning interest.

As a result, Pump & Paddle will probably not be able to keep serving customers and employees well enough to survive. As other profitable companies improve, Pump & Paddle will fall further and further behind the competition. The profitless Pump & Paddle will gradually lose both customers and employees to other profitable companies that are improving, and will end up unable to serve anybody effectively.

On the other hand, if Pump & Paddle does make profit in its initial years — enough profit — it will be able to keep improving its products for customers and creating jobs for employees, and it will remain competitive. By making high net profit, the company will be able to collect a good deal of extra cash from customers. Its high profitability will also probably enable it to raise more cash from investors; the profit will be evidence that it is probably capable of using additional investment to make even more profit and thus pay high future dividends on present investment.

The more profit the company makes, the more it can improve its products and jobs, thus better serving its customers and employees.

•

In fact, a company's very pursuit of profit forces the company to serve customers and employees as well as it can. This gives both customers and employees an extremely powerful and effective form of democratic control over the company. To keep increasing profit, a company generally has to keep increasing its sales, which usually requires continued expansion and improvement of the products and services it offers to customers. And to keep increasing profit a company generally also has to keep increasing its employment in order to deliver more and better products and services, which usually requires continued expansion and improvement of the jobs it offers to employees.

Each day, by choosing which companies' products and services to buy, all the customers are in effect voting on each company's products and services. By starting or keeping or leaving jobs, employees are in effect voting on each company's jobs. In a very real way, each company's pursuit of profit amounts to its striving to win more votes from both customers and employees. The profit system is really a superbly efficient system for automatically forcing and guiding each company to serve all its outsider groups as well as possible — because, as the financial picture shows, that is just what a company has to do to keep getting from all the outsider groups what it needs to keep increasing its profit.

•

In the preceding chapter, where we looked at company finances from the stockholders' viewpoint, we saw that a company that can earn only low profit relative to investment will best serve its stockholders by using all or most of the value gain from net profit for paying dividends. But a company that can earn very high profit relative to investment will best serve its stockholders by paying them only relatively low dividends and using most of its profit for investment.

And we saw that in fact companies generally do operate according to this rule. As a rule, less profitable companies generally use relatively more of their profit for dividends and less for investment; the more profitable companies usually use relatively less for dividends and more for investment. Most of this investment involves improving and expanding products for customers and jobs for employees, in competition for increased future profit.

As a result, high profit means just the opposite of less for customers and employees and more for owners: *high profit means* MORE *invested to improve and increase products and jobs for customers and employees, with* LESS *paid to the owners as dividends.* In other words, high profit doesn't just mean the company has more available to improve its products and jobs; it also means the company probably will use a higher *percentage* of the higher profit for these purposes and will pay a lower percentage to the owners. The owners want the company to keep and invest the profit for these purposes in hopes of getting higher profit and dividends later.

•

Considering the extent to which our historical economic progress and our present economy are based on the profit system, and the logic and simplicity of the financial system for measuring and reporting profit, there is a dreadful lack of even elementary understanding of profit, and this lack is reflected in most of the public dialogue about profit that we read and hear. Much of the condemnation of "high" profit that issues from supposedly well-informed political leaders, and from most of the media, is simply unfounded, because the speaker or writer neglected to take the basic step of measuring the profit relative to investment to determine whether the profit *is* high. Most public statements for or against high profit — even those from business leaders and politicians who speak in favor of profit — seem based on the entirely erroneous supposition that high profit means more money for company owners and less for everybody else.

Almost all public talk about high profit requires examination. First, compare the company's net profit to its equity to see if its profit *is* high. If possible look at the return-on-equity average and trend over several years, not just the number for a single year, to filter out the short-term ups and downs.

Second, bear in mind that high net profit is good for the customers and employees and society in general, for a host of reasons. Profit is value the company has created and added to the economy, value that it rather than its owners receives cash for, value that it needs to keep improving its products for customers and jobs for employees. The higher a company's profit, the more it can — and probably will — improve its products for customers and jobs for employees; and if a company's profit is particularly high relative to its investment, it will probably use more of its profit to improve products and jobs and less to pay dividends to its owners.